"Rick Stedman understands we are emotional [...] emotional God, and that some of our deepest, [...] come when we connect with him at an emotio[...] and Rick takes us on an amazing journey. Your prayer life will never be the same."

Gene Appel, Senior Pastor
Eastside Christian Church, Anaheim, California

"The potential impact of this book is huge. Learning to relate with God emotionally through prayer, the Psalms, and the psychology of attachment theory is a brilliant way for readers to experience spiritual and relational transformation. I wish all Christians would learn to live and pray this way—especially Christian counselors and pastors."

Kenneth Logan, PsyD
Professor of Counseling
Western Seminary, Portland, Oregon

"The Psalms, as John Calvin told us, is a mirror of the soul and helps us understand and express our emotions in ways that draw us closer to God. I recommend this book with great enthusiasm. Rick Stedman is an able guide to help us tap into this God-given resource for life-changing prayer."

Tremper Longman III
Robert H. Gundry Professor of Biblical Studies
Westmont College

"I have read dozens of books on prayer and *Praying the Psalms* is the best book on prayer that I have read in a very long time. Rick has discovered an untapped gold mine by exploring the emotional insights in the Psalms. The book is both refreshing and probing. *Praying the Psalms* is refreshing because it looks through the largely unexplored lens of the emotions in the Psalms. I found this invaluable and extremely well-researched! The book is also probing because it challenges the reader to experience a deeper and more emotionally satisfying prayer relationship with God. *Praying the Psalms* is the next book on prayer everyone should read!"

Steve Bond, Senior Pastor
Summit Christian Church, Reno, Nevada

"In *Praying the Psalms* I found Rick Stedman's transparency to be refreshing, especially in the area of relationships. My wife and I found many launching points for deep spiritual conversation. I am currently doing a series of sermons in Psalms and have found this to be my most helpful resource."

Ken Long, Senior Pastor
Northshore Christian Church, Everett, Washington

"The Psalms can be an intimidating. After all, there are 150 of them! Where do you start? What are they trying to say? How are we to process all of these various expressions of emotion in a clear way? Rick Stedman has written a resource to help us see not only what the Psalms say, but what they have to convey about an emotional God who desires to connect to you and me as emotional beings. The contents are refreshingly transparent, insightful, and extremely practical. If you've ever struggled with prayer (and we all have), or ever wondered how to practically apply the Psalms, you will find both encouragement and tangible steps to immediately put into practice."

Aaron Brockett, Senior Pastor
Traders Point Christian Church, Indianapolis, Indiana

"Does being a good Christian mean that we can't allow ourselves to feel certain emotions? *Praying the Psalms* challenges our notions about what we feel and how we express those feelings to God in prayer. This book will change the way you understand and relate to God, so if you've been looking for an upgrade in your prayer life, this book is for you!"

Erik Neilson, Senior Pastor
Adventure Christian Church, McMinnville, Oregon

"If the Psalms are a 'gymnasium for the soul,' as St. Ambrose called them, you'll find no better personal spiritual trainer than Pastor Rick Stedman. Those yearning for deeper connection with God and the wholeness that brings will find what they're looking for in this deeply practical book."

Brian Jones, author of *Second Guessing God* and *Forgiveness*
Senior Pastor, Christ's Church of the Valley, Royersford, Pennsylvania

"I am so excited for Rick Stedman's call for us to emotionally connect with God! I have found that much of what is called Christianity is in reality a cold, emotionless, stoic philosophy that is built on knowledge rather than love. Rick's book will show you the way to connect with God by *Praying the Psalms* and in doing so you will have a vibrant and real love relationship with the One who loves you most."

Chuck Booher, Senior Pastor
Crossroads Christian Church, Corona, California

"In *Praying the Psalms*, Rick Stedman has harnessed the important principle of 'Emotional Intelligence' in our relationship with God and others from a biblical perspective—thus, TRUTH. For anyone going though life transitions or who just wants to deepen relationships, this book will be a useful tool in effective navigation."

Roger Storms, Lead Pastor
Chandler Christian Church, Chandler, Arizona

PRAYING
THE
PSALMS

RICK
STEDMAN

HARVEST HOUSE PUBLISHERS
EUGENE, OREGON

Cover by Knail, Salem, Oregon

Back cover author photo by Jodi Burgess

Published in association with Books & Such Management, 52 Mission Circle, Suite 122, PMB 170, Santa Rosa, CA 95409-5370, www.booksandsuch.com.

PRAYING THE PSALMS

Copyright © 2016 Rick Stedman
Published by Harvest House Publishers
Eugene, Oregon 97402
www.harvesthousepublishers.com

ISBN 978-0-7369-6073-1 (pbk.)
ISBN 978-0-7369-6074-8 (eBook)

Library of Congress Cataloging-in-Publication Data
Names: Stedman, Rick, author.
Title: Praying the Psalms / Rick Stedman.
Description: Eugene, Oregon : Harvest House Publishers, 2016.
Identifiers: LCCN 2016019463 (print) | LCCN 2016021437 (ebook) | ISBN 9780736960731 (pbk.) | ISBN 9780736960748 ()
Subjects: LCSH: Bible. Psalms—Criticism, interpretation, etc. | Bible. Psalms—Devotional use. | Bible. Psalms, I-X—Criticism, interpretation, etc. | Bible. Psalms, I-X—Devotional use.
Classification: LCC BS1430.54 .S73 2016 (print) | LCC BS1430.54 (ebook) | DDC 223/.206—dc23
LC record available at https://lccn.loc.gov/2016019463

Printed in the United States of America

16 17 18 19 20 21 22 23 24 / BP-CD / 10 9 8 7 6 5 4 3 2 1

To the precious people of Adventure Christian Church, Roseville, California:
Whom I was honored to serve as senior pastor for twenty-one years,
who changed the landscape of eternity through their sacrifice and service,
and among whom are many we count as our dearest friends.

And to Lori Clark, my administrative assistant for nineteen years:
Who has the greatest servant's heart of anyone I've ever known,
who is a humble yet mighty prayer warrior,
and who, I sometimes wonder, may be an angel in disguise.

CONTENTS

1

Our Need for Emotional Closeness with God and Others

Introduction to the Psalms

———————— ❧ ————————

"The psalmists are angry people."[1]—Eugene Petersen

I awoke angry.

As my emotions from the previous night came back full throttle, I saw her sleeping in the bed beside me and thought, *There she is—that woman. I'm so mad at her!*

The sleeping woman was, of course, my wife. The night before we had slipped into a fight just before bed, so I went to sleep angry.

Yes, yes, I know the Bible says, "Do not let the sun go down while you are still angry." I am a pastor, after all. But I was mad—really mad—so I climbed into bed and rationalized my behavior. *Well, the sun is already down so it's too late to apply that verse tonight anyway. I'll just go to sleep mad and deal with this before the sun sets tomorrow.*

As the new day dawned, I lay there with my head on the pillow and allowed the pain of the past to cripple an otherwise bright, innocent new morning. Deep in my heart I knew that I should forgive her and put the past behind me, but instead I chose to fan the embers of my anger into flame: *Oh, she makes me so mad sometimes. Soooo mad!*

Then it hit me—I couldn't remember why I was mad.

Think, Rick, think! Come on, you can do it. You've got to remember. What did she do that made you so mad?

I gave this question my full attention, as much as if I were a contestant during Final Jeopardy. It was important; otherwise I couldn't justify and continue to nurse my anger.

It took some time and effort, but finally the content of the argument came back to me. As it turned out, the actual issue wasn't a big deal, but as you and I both know, issues don't always need to be significant in order to qualify as fight material. Once the minor issue we fought over was identified, I was able to get out of bed, self-righteously smug and strangely pleased to be angry again.

Physically Mature, Emotionally Childish

Pleased to be angry? Yes, I admit it. Mea culpa. I was angry and I liked it. At that moment, I had more in common with children who cling to their toys than a mature adult who realizes that anger is nothing to play with.

I wish I could tell you that the above story was the exception rather than the rule, but at that time in my life I was angry often, most of it due to church problems. After ten tremendous years during which our church grew in size from zero to over five thousand, we entered a time of severe trials and went through a nasty church split. I made some serious leadership errors, and others reneged on big promises and misbehaved in various ways. I became confused, hurt, and—above all—angry.

I was angry with friends who betrayed me. Angry at former church members who were spreading false rumors. Angry at the nefarious one for dividing our church family (the root meaning of *demon* in Greek is "to divide"). Angry with myself for not being a better leader, and angry for being angry. And as I have already admitted, from time to time I took my anger out on my precious wife and kids. In short, I was mad at just about everybody.

I was even angry at God.

> "Whatever else Christianity may be, it is a set of emotions."
> —Robert C. Roberts[2]

What a mess. I was smoldering with unhealthy anger and knew it was wrong. I was irate and unable to let go of the cancerous emotion.

What was wrong with me? Here I was a middle-aged, healthy man, married for over twenty-five years to a wonderful wife and the father of three great kids, founder and senior pastor of a successful megachurch, and had a doctorate in spiritual formation. I was blessed beyond measure, knew the Bible inside and out, and spent plenty of time in the spiritual disciplines such as prayer, Bible study, worship, and fasting. I knew the right things to do—and was even doing them.

Yet I was messed up emotionally. In prayer, I truly forgave those who had wounded me, but the painful memories would still accost my mind unbidden. I went to counselors and poured out my heart, but the sadness and hurt would not heal. I went to prayer meetings and asked seasoned prayer-champions to pray for inner healing, but the feelings remained. I read books galore, filling my mind with biblical and practical information, but was unable to mend the brokenness inside.

Where could I find healing for my heart and rest for my spirit?

The Wake-Up Call

By this point, dear reader, you may be confused. You may have started this book thinking it was about praying the emotions in the Psalms, which—be assured—it is.

What Is Prayer?

"Prayer is nothing more than an ongoing and growing love relationship with God the Father, Son, and Holy Spirit." —Richard Foster[3]

"The difference between talking about praying and praying is the same as the difference between blowing a kiss and kissing."—G.K. Chesterton[4]

But before we explore the vast emotional terrain of the Psalms and unpack how praying them helps us grow in emotional health—which has the power to improve *all* of our relationships—I feel it necessary to tell you my story of emotional awakening. So, I continue…

My emotional unrest ebbed and flowed for almost a decade. Then, after twenty-one years of leading the church I founded and loved, I felt God's clarion call that it was time for a change for both the church and me. At the same time, God called a pastor to be my successor and arranged a seamless transition. Suddenly, I was free to begin a new chapter in my life. And since Amy and I were also recent empty nesters, I thought we both would enjoy a new season of life together.

I was wrong. Life together wasn't as much fun as I had anticipated; surprisingly, we began fighting a lot. Little things seemed to be big irritants, and we fell into a rut of arguing. Our biggest arguments were of the "he said, she said" variety. "Why did you say such and such?" "I didn't say that!" "Yes you did!" "No, I didn't!" And on and on. We were riding what could be called a *misery*-go-round. Life was not pleasant in the Stedman household.

Fortunately, we had a rock-solid marriage based on our commitment to Christ, a deep and lasting love for one another, and a resolution never to consider divorce. But we were not happy.

So we decided to find a Christian therapist who was not affiliated with our church. While researching counselors, a phrase on a website caught my eye: *emotionally focused therapy*.

I knew in an instant that was the ticket for us.

Our problem was not the result of financial or health pressures. Neither of us had been unfaithful or abusive. And we weren't suffering from an alcohol or drug addiction. We just were not being nice to each other and were hurting each other emotionally. Or so I thought.

What the therapy revealed was a shocking and awful truth: my wife and I were almost completely disconnected emotionally. What a wake-up call!

I'm a pretty rational guy (actually, very rational), which I come by naturally and by training in philosophy. Plus, I'm fairly independent (okay, again the truth is that I'm very independent) and self-sufficient. Finally, I'm a tinkerer and home handyman who likes the challenge of fixing something that's broken.

But I could not fix our marriage and I certainly couldn't fix my emotionally shutdown wife.

She needed an emotionally present husband, one who willingly shared his feelings, vulnerabilities, and needs. But I was a logical, self-sufficient, Mr. Fix-it. Of course, I enjoyed spending time with my wife and kids—especially when we were doing some project or task together. I thought I was a pretty good husband and father. I was happy when with them, but also happy to spend time alone, surrounded by my books, tools, and tasks.

The years of church stress had pushed me inward, and I had become a rather solitary man emotionally. I embodied what Paul Simon wrote about in his 1965 megahit (with Art Garfunkel) "I Am a Rock." I had my armor on 24/7. Sheesh—in graduate school my best friend even nicknamed me Rock.

But that was not good for my wife or me. Once the kids left for college, we were left with an emotional vacuum at home, which, I am learning, is a lifestyle that leaves everyone feeling empty.

The Greatest Discovery of All

Though my wife loves me deeply, it hit me like a ton of bricks that she was profoundly unhappy in this one aspect of our marriage.

So I began a journey toward emotional self-discovery.

The more I was able to tune in to her emotions, do the same with my own, and—here's the crucial part—share with her my inner feelings, she felt *connected* with me. She felt loved by me. And as she learned to connect emotionally with me, I felt loved by her. Thankfully, due to this deeper sense of emotional connection, our marriage turned a fast corner back toward health. Together we began to learn about and grow toward emotional maturity.

And after experiencing the tremendous importance of emotional connection in marriage, my eyes were opened to its value in other relationships: family, friends, church, and workplace.

Then it hit me. Could the same be true in my relationship with God? Was emotional connection a missing ingredient in my Christian walk?

It probably will not surprise you to hear that my experience with God to this point in my life was mostly cerebral rather than emotional. My faith was rock-solid, my prayer life active, and I believed in the closeness (theologians call this "immanence") of God. I knew and treasured Jesus' promise, "I am with you always" (Matthew 28:20). [5] But to be candid, in hindsight it now seems to me that I believed in God's closeness more than I felt it. And I wondered how God felt about me.

Did God consider our relationship to be an intimate one? Did God *feel loved*[6] by me? Truth to be told, probably not.

Wait, you may be thinking, *does God have feelings? Is God an* emotional *being?*

The short answer, biblically, is a resounding yes! The long answer will unfold in the rest of this book as we will learn about the rich and varied emotions of God. The God revealed in the Bible, in fact, is extremely passionate. He loves and hates, rejoices and grieves, laughs and laments. Emotions are a part of who God is and how he made us. Of course, as pastor Peter Scazzero cautions, emotions should neither be worshipped nor denied. [7] The Psalms strike the perfect balance: they remind us to feel grief, anger, sadness, joy, and envy—that is, to feel a broad range of emotions. Yet, at the same time, only God is worshipped—never the emotions, the worshipper, or even the Bible itself.

A Journey Toward Emotional Maturity

How does a rational, analytic, left-brained guy like me learn about emotions? Well, from books, of course. So I gathered all the books in my library that dealt with emotions and I read everything our counselor suggested. These in turn led to others, still others, and so forth.

In my research, another surprise unfolded: authors who dealt insightfully with the importance of emotions seemed to fall into four main groupings, four independent schools of thought that were focused on the reality and value of emotions. I came to call these four clusters: *streams of emotional insight.* Here are the first three streams that struck me in their similarity:

- Emotional Intelligence
- Emotionally Focused Therapy
- Emotionally Healthy Spirituality

Each of these streams provided me volumes of information, case studies, and understanding. As I read book after book and study upon study, I felt like I was drinking from a fire hose. I was simply overwhelmed with the profundity and practicality of this information. It was life-changing. I came to see that emotional expertise helps one excel at, well, *everything.* For instance:

- Emotional intelligence is the number one predictor of career success.
- Emotional connection is the key ingredient in marital satisfaction.
- Emotional health is a crucial component of spiritual maturity.

In the course of this book, I will unpack and illustrate each of these emphases. Their own stories are remarkable, their founders true trailblazers, and their lessons easily transferrable.

Their combined insights are so valuable, so revolutionary, that I wish I had learned them years ago. It saddens me to reflect on the things that might have been had I been more emotionally astute:

conflicts resolved, successes achieved, and friendships maintained. But it also inspired me to look ahead to the ways that emotional health will benefit me and those I love in the years ahead. I am not one to cry over spilt milk; I tend not to gaze upon the past but instead look ahead to avoiding such spills in the future. (Yes, discerning reader, the fact that I tend not to cry over spilt milk also reveals my general dislike of crying, but more on that in a later chapter.)

In short, I want to shout from the mountaintops the insights I have learned about emotional maturity. If everyone could grow in emotional maturity, the world would be a better place. Churches would be healthier. Marriages would be stronger and children more secure. People would feel more connected with friends and family. Christians would feel closer to God. I'm no utopian idealist, so I am not implying this will solve all the world's problems. But it may solve lots of them, which is why this book and others about emotional maturity are worth the effort.

The Fourth Stream of Emotional Insight

You, dear reader, may be slightly irritated and confused because the fourth stream of emotional insight was not mentioned in the previous section. Like a seventh note that was left unresolved or a sentence that was not..., you may have been bothered that I listed there only three of the four streams. Why have I delayed identifying the fourth stream? The answer is: simply for emphasis, as the fourth stream of emotional insight is the focus of this book. Here it is:

- Praying the Psalms Emotionally

I was shocked to realize that the best book for developing emotional maturity was in my Bible all along. For decades I read from the Bible every day, patterned my life after its principles, and made teaching from it my career. However, I totally missed the emotional power of this gem—right in the middle of my all-time favorite book, the Bible. I carried it with me under my arm but failed to connect it with my heart. In essence, *emotional maturity can be learned by praying the Psalms.*

Praying Scripture:

"The most intriguing thing to me was [the instructor's] description of a simple prayer practice that in all my journey and reading I had never heard before—the power of praying Scripture…Using Psalm 71, we were instructed to go back and forth, verse by verse, praying the Psalm. We could use phrases from the verse and add to them, or simply pray the verse almost word for word. It was wonderful. That simple lesson opened up whole new worlds for me."[8]—Jonathan Graf

"God has handed us two sticks of dynamite with which to demolish our strongholds: His Word and prayer. What is more powerful than two sticks of dynamite placed in separate locations? Two strapped together. [Praying God's Word] is taking our two primary sticks of dynamite—prayer and the Word—strapping them together, and igniting them with faith in what God says He can do."[9]—Beth Moore

---

The book of Psalms is one of sixty-six books within the Bible, and none of these books is more saturated with emotions than the Psalms. No book more broad or inclusive in the types of emotions it addresses. No book whose writers are more honest with their emotions. It is a truly remarkable, unique book in the canon. As John Calvin wrote, "I have been wont to call this book not inappropriately, an anatomy of all parts of the soul; for there is not an emotion of which anyone can be conscious that is not here represented as in a mirror."[10] In other words, as we read and pray the Psalms, we see ourselves emotionally. As David Allan Hubbard put this, "The Psalms speak to all seasons of our souls."[11] Plus, I knew that Jesus prayed the Psalms.[12]

Before my wake-up call, I had read the Psalms countless times and preached dozens of sermons on them. I had prayed through them for a couple of years straight and had led our church in doing the same. These were edifying experiences for us, to be sure. But I sense now that I had blinders on, blinders that kept me from noticing the *emotional focus* of the Psalms.

In the Psalms, emotions are everywhere. Few Psalms lack an emotional word or context, and many are just bursting with emotion. As I began to pay attention to emotional words and phrases in the Psalms, I was overwhelmed by their intensity and frequency. David and the other psalmists were emotionally expressive—often bluntly and excessively so. Listen to these typical verses:

- "Happy are those who..." (Psalm 1:1 NRSV).
- "Why do the nations conspire, and the peoples plot in vain?" (Psalm 2:1).
- "LORD, how many are my foes!" (Psalm 3:1).
- "Answer me when I call, O God...in distress" (Psalm 4:1 NRSV).
- "Listen to my words, LORD, consider my lament" (Psalm 5:1).

Thus begin the first 5 Psalms, and we still have 145 to go!

As I focused on the emotional condition of the authors of the Psalms, I often had the impression that I was looking in a mirror. These writers were angry yet hopeful, worried but also trusting. They were able to find joy in spite of struggles, and usually able to turn laments into praise. They were wounded worshippers who reminded me a lot—of me. I too wanted to be happy, yet was saddened by the sorrows of life. I too frequently called out to God in distress, begged him to hear my pleas, and wondered whether God was angry with me. The Psalms were like a looking glass, reflecting my own soul.

In effect, the Psalms showed me that I wasn't alone. I wasn't a bad person or a spiritual failure for feeling what I felt. The emotions I experienced were typical, maybe even to be expected. Otherwise, why would they be in the Bible?

And I discovered that the emotional elements in the Psalms are powerful, formative, and curative—when used in prayer.

Learning to Share Our Feelings with God:

"Many of us often do not feel like praying. But we do feel many other things. We feel sad, angry, relieved, joyful, anxious, puzzled. To pray, all we need to do is harness that emotional energy as fuel that lifts our prayers, and ourselves, to God...Turning the inner dialogue up to God involves sharing with him our actual thoughts and feelings, listening to the underlying attitudes of ourselves and others (whether of pride, or its cousin, self-pity), and listening to God's answer to what is going on within. Much of the Psalms is the account of the Psalmist's inner dialogue coming out—and going up to God. It is a vital way of staying connected to God."
—Robert Warren [13]

Connecting with God and Others—Through Prayer

This is why it is so valuable to *pray* the Psalms. As we will discuss in later chapters, the heart of emotional intelligence, emotionally focused therapy, and emotionally focused spirituality is this: emotions are the language of love and relationships. They are the oxygen by which relationships breathe and thrive. Thus, here is the core conviction of this book: *deep connections with others require emotional communication—and nowhere is this more exemplified than in the Psalms.*

This is what my wife and I were missing from each other: emotional awareness, sharing, and vulnerability. Psychologists call this *affective communication. Affective* is a psychological term that describes anything that relates to emotions, attitudes, feelings, or moods. In other words, my wife and I were both thirsting for deeper emotional interaction with one another: compassion, attention, openness, and feeling-centered dialogue.

> Prayer is indeed a relational event. As pastor and author Ray Stedman wrote, "Prayer is God the Son praying to God the Father in the power of God the Spirit, and the prayer room is the believer's heart."[14] Or as David Adam put this, "The prayers of the saints are affairs of the heart."[15]

Real closeness between two people requires an open exchange of affective content. We have to trust each other with our inner feelings, concerns, and desires. We share the good, the bad, and the ugly. We laugh and cry and get mad together. We feel safe and valued. The net result is a deep sense of interpersonal connection, which is a pretty good way to define love.

In short, love requires emotional communication, which is why praying the Psalms is such a powerful way to deepen our relationship with God. To become not just believers but belongers. Friends rather than merely followers. People who know God rather than those who only know about God. At the risk of sounding oversentimental, we can become lovers of God.

The concept of a love relationship with God is not new. For example, many of our church hymns and choruses are about loving God: "O Love That Will Not Let Me Go," "Love Divine," "I Keep Falling in Love with You," "Your Love Never Fails," and possibly the best-known song in all Christendom, "Jesus Loves Me." Though I have sung these songs and others like them countless times, they have always felt a little off target for me, a tad too sentimental. I'm sure I'm not the only one who has felt this. I knew rationally that God loved me and I loved him, but I seldom felt comfortable emoting about my love for him. Nonetheless, I tried to sing the songs with gusto, even though I didn't experience them as a perfect fit. As a worship-pastor friend of mine used to say, "We Christians don't tell lies; we sing them." He was speaking of songs like "I Surrender All," but his point applies also to songs about loving God. In my experience, evangelicals sing about loving God better than they experience it.

But when my eyes were opened to the depth and frequency of emotional dialogue with God in the Psalms, and when I began to pray the Psalms with an emphasis of identifying emotions and talking about those with God, I began to feel closer to God. More attuned. Connected. All in all, it felt like—love. Yes, praying the Psalms led me into deeper friendship and intimacy with God.

Psalms is often called the prayer book of the Bible but, in evangelical circles, it is usually read more than prayed. This is unfortunate, because praying the Psalms is a terrific tool for soul-making.

Praying the Psalms is like a no-holds-barred, mixed-martial-arts emotional battle with God. Of course, God always wins, but the process changes us for the better. The Psalms are not church-lady approved, sanitized prayers. They are real, edgy, and authentic—even violent at times. In praying the Psalms, we learn to face our deepest hopes, hurts, and fears and to bring them to God in brutally honest prayer. We learn to identify and express a wide range of emotions, while at the same time keeping those emotions from ruling our lives. We learn how to handle hate and anger, overcome guilt and sorrow, and experience grace and mercy. After all, the only place to learn these skills is within real relationships, which is very clever of God.

In the process, we find intimacy with God, deeper community with others, and—in what is perhaps the biggest surprise of all—we discover our very selves.

When we pray the Psalms, we deepen our relationship with God and form a secure attachment with him. In turn, this gives us a stable, affirming base from which we can move out into the world. We can explore, experiment, and face new challenges, all because we have a solid connection with God in the center of our lives. In addition, this solid, secure attachment base with God is a platform from which we can venture forth to deepen our love for friends and family. Praying the Psalms allows God not just to inform our minds but also to transform our hearts and relationships.

Blessings Among the Battles:

"In truth, nothing can overcome the blessing of God on our lives even though he permits us to face battles along the way." —Jim Cymbala[16]

Is God Smart Enough to Set the Agenda for Our Daily Prayers?

Consider the emotional impact of praying just the first few words from Psalm 120:

> I call on the LORD in my distress,
>   and he answers me.
> Save me, LORD,
>   from lying lips,
>   and from deceitful tongues.
>   (Psalm 120:1-2)

As we pray this Psalm with a focus on emotions, we immediately are confronted with the feeling word *distress*.

So we open our minds and spirits to this issue. Might God want to talk with us, on this particular day, about some current problem that is causing distress in our lives? We pause on the first line and present ourselves before God, praying slowly and repeatedly, *"I call on the Lord in my distress, I call on the Lord in my distress..."* If we need to, we pause in prayerful silence for a few moments. As Kathleen Norris said, "Silence is not passive…it has the power to change you."[17] As we pray, we search our hearts for any current problem that is causing us distress. We meditate on the word *distress, distress, distress.* In effect we are asking God, *"Lord, you brought this issue up. Now reveal to me the* distress *that you would like us to deal with today in prayer."* (This is a simplified form of what monks call *lectio divina.*)

It may be a medical issue that we are fearful about, a problem one of our kids is going through, a worry about our financial future, or a million other concerns. Rare is the person who will not have at least one source of distress in life, one thorn in the flesh (or barb in the soul) at any given time. In a world like ours, there's a lot to be distressed about.

But many of us ignore, swallow, or deny our emotions of stress and distress, thinking that to focus on them reveals a lack of faith or spiritual immaturity. Praying this Psalm reveals to us that the opposite is true: it takes maturity to be self-aware and faith to be confident that God cares about little stuff like this. Plus, sharing on an emotional level with God, believing that he cares enough for us to listen attentively to our pleas, strengthens the attachment bond between the Lord and us.

So we can express the source of our distress to God. For the author of this Psalm, the source of his distress was the lying and deceit of others.

"Save me, LORD, from lying lips and from deceitful tongues" (Psalm 120:2).

The psalmist identifies the source of his distress (liars) and asks God to save him from those hurtful actions and people. So let's think about this personally. Have you ever been hurt by the lies of others, injured by the false words of a friend? I certainly have, and this Psalm is a perfect chance to discuss with God those inner wounds.

But don't move too quickly from the psalmist's issue, because if we rest and meditate upon it, often we uncover a feeling or concern that was lying slightly below our consciousness. We might find a huge surprise: the Psalms often read as if God is addressing them to our very circumstances. It's as if God has been reading our mail and eavesdropping on the inner conversations of our heart.

In an awesome show of omniscience and time-transcendence, God often arranges the reading of the Psalm to coincide with the exact day it is needed. It is likely that on the very day we turn to pray Psalm 120 in our sequential journey of praying the Psalms, the issue causing our distress might be deception. Maybe some lies have been told about us. Or it could be lies that we are telling ourselves. Either way, we can take these to God in prayer, meditate over them in conversation with God, and seek his healing touch and counsel as to how we should deal with this problem.

On the other hand, after deep reflection we may conclude that the lies of others are not our current source of misery. Instead, our distress might have a different cause, such as fear, worry, or betrayal. So we modify the prayer accordingly: *Save me, O Lord, from worry and from the anxiety that is causing me such distress. Right now I'm worried about [list worries here], and these worries are making my life miserable.*

Let me give a personal example. During a difficult time in our church, one key leader repeatedly assured me, "Don't worry, Rick. I've got your back." He must have said this over a dozen times. Then the blow of betrayal came. In a crucial meeting where I was not present, he not only failed to defend me but he sided with those who opposed me. Later that evening, I phoned him and said, "I've got to ask, what does 'I've got your back' mean to you? It certainly means something different to me than what you did today." The next day he resigned from his leadership position and abruptly left the church.

His betrayal and abandonment distressed me deeply. The only way I was able to carry on was because of the firm support of my wife, family and friends, other leaders, and, of course, prayer.

Like the psalmist, it is appropriate to pray about our distresses. Like talking to a therapist or close confidant, we may not resolve the issue, but at least we will feel better because we have opened the wound for inspection and cleansing. It now has a chance to heal, more so, at least, than if it were left hidden and infected.

As we pray with special attention to emotions, we interact with God as the ultimate confidant, the supreme counselor (as the Holy Spirit is described in John 14:16) to whom we can take all of our emotions, our triumphs and struggles, and our joys and sorrows. As we pray the Psalms, we learn that God not only welcomes such emotional talk—he picks the topics! He schedules the counseling agenda. God is no Rogerian therapist, simply listening to and reflecting back upon whatever issue we choose to discuss. God is proactive in the Psalms; he sets the daily prayer themes, which in Psalm 120 includes distress, deception, hate, and peace.

I hope the example of Psalm 120:1-2 whets your appetite to pray the Psalms. Those two verses are a helpful example of how we can connect deeply with God through praying the Psalms—and learn tons about ourselves to boot. Plus, there are 2459 more emotionally laden verses to go, which will lead us toward emotional and spiritual maturity.

Athanasius on the Psalms:

"He who recites the Psalms is uttering [them] as his own words, and each sings them as if they were written concerning him…[H]e handles them as if he is speaking about himself. And the things spoken are such that he lifts them up to God as himself acting and speaking them from himself."—Athanasius[18]

Should We Pray the Psalms Thematically or Sequentially?

Praying the Psalms is entering God's graduate school of emotional maturity, God's advanced course for interpersonal attachment. Doing so deepens our relationship with God, but also has the potential to draw us closer with family, friends, and even ourselves.

How should we go about praying the Psalms with special attention on emotional attunement with God? There are two basic options: pray the Psalms in sequential order or find a Psalm that expresses the emotion we are feeling each day.

As a daily spiritual discipline, I suggest the former method. Of course, the latter method is not a bad practice, and it certainly is better than not praying at all. For instance, during times of intense fear it is very helpful to pray Psalm 23, and during times of abundant blessing and thankfulness, it is helpful to pray Psalm 136.

But this pick-and-choose method, if followed exclusively, tends to trap us in our emotional ruts and limits our emotional scope. For instance, in times of grief it is helpful to pray Psalms of lament, which give voice to our sorrow and help us feel less alone in our pain. (This cures what has been called "the costly loss of lament" [19] in our culture and churches.) But choosing to exclusively pray the Psalms of lament, day after day, might unnecessarily lengthen the tenure of that negative emotion. We could be stuck in grief and sorrow for months.

On the other hand, praying the Psalms sequentially has several advantages. God does not allow us to linger too long in any one emotion, and we are forced to pray across a broader spectrum of feelings. We will notice quickly that a Psalm of lament might be followed by one of gratitude or two of joy. They seem to be haphazardly organized, the emotions jumping all over the place—like real life! But this seemingly random order carries an added benefit. By allowing God to choose the order of the Psalms, we will be confronted by emotions that we may not choose on our own, and maybe even some that we haven't consciously dealt with in our own lives.

Actually, it's a pretty wild ride. The Psalms are not a philosophical or psychological analysis of emotions, nor a systematized exploration of our passions and feelings. There is no order to the arrangement of these emotions at all. They can turn on a dime. Upset at God in one verse and praising him in the next. Overjoyed, and then suddenly depressed. We can get dizzy if we are not careful.

This is why, as Eugene Peterson suggests, the Psalms are best experienced by praying them in the order they appear in the Bible. [20] At first glance it might seem logical to group all of the praises together, then the doubts, followed by laments, and so on. Some books or studies may approach the Psalms in this manner. After all, this is how scholarship is done in Western civilization. Like a frog in a lab class, we take an organic whole, slice and dice it, group similar parts together, and study the parts in a more orderly fashion (as if God hadn't ordered frogs well originally). We end up with lots of interesting information, but the frog is dead.

Of all the books in the Bible, slicing, dicing, and reorganizing the Psalms can stifle the emotional life found within. So I recommend the daily practice of praying the Psalms, one at a time, in the order given in the Bible. Eventually, we discover that God uses the seemingly haphazard order of the Psalms to help us deal with the disorder of our lives. Notice the emotions and try to *feel* the Psalms as you go.

A Four-Step Process for Praying the Psalms

Therefore, our plan in this book is to pray the first ten Psalms sequentially and emotionally. Through this, you will learn methods that you can follow on your own to pray the rest of the Psalms. We will also pray them slowly and meditatively, not worried about maintaining a certain pace.

The *first* step in our approach is to simply pray a Psalm by reading it aloud to God, word-for-word as it appears in the Bible, and searching for emotional words and phrases during this first go-through.

It is paramount that, as we pray, we read the Psalm aloud and with emotion. If you are tempted to skip this oral step (because our common method of personal reading is to read silently), please don't give in. Too often the Bible is read in our minds alone. Though this is better than not reading the Bible at all, mental-only reading tends to tame the Bible's emotional tongue and dull its rhetorical edge. Plus, there are many other positive benefits to reading and praying aloud. (For further discussion about these, see the second book in this prayer trilogy, *Praying the Promises of Jesus.*[21])

As I pray, I sometimes find it helpful to imagine that I am an actor on a stage, reading a script with passion—facial gestures and body language that convey emotions seem to spontaneously appear. When we pray aloud in this manner, we allow the words to form in our throats and mouths and then flow across our lips. With practice, we can almost taste the emotions, such as the sweetness of grace and the bitterness of regret. We can feel them in our faces and bodies. Because the Psalms are passionate poems, it is a travesty to read them robotically, as if they were assembly directions for some household appliance. Read and pray them with gusto and feeling. Put your heart into it; the psalmists certainly did.

Our goal in this first step is to search for affective or emotionally laden words or phrases. As we pray, I suggest we circle or highlight such word(s) during the first read-through. If the Psalm is long, we can choose to stop after a few verses, marking the point at which we will begin anew tomorrow.

Second, we list these words on a separate piece of paper or in a journal (see appendix 1 for an example of each step in this process).

Third, we prayerfully reflect on each of the emotional words we listed in the previous step and add comments next to those words as to how they relate to our daily lives or to the lives of those we love.

Last, we weave the emotional words and comments from step three into a prayer to our heavenly Father, who longs to connect and attune with us on an emotional level. (This too is illustrated in appendix 1.)

In this final step we pray the Psalm again, but this time as if we were the psalmist, writing about the issues in our own lives. This is easy to do because most Psalms are written in the first person. Those that are in the third person (or the rare second person) can easily be adapted into first.

In this final step we pray through the Psalm, consciously pausing and alighting on the emotional words, asking God, *"Which part of this Psalm do you want me to pray through today?"* There is no need to spend equal amounts of time on every verse. In time, as we pray through all 150 Psalms over and over again, there will be ample opportunity to emphasize different verses.

The point is to find, each day, something emotionally significant to discuss with God.

Praying the Psalms for Emotional Attunement with God

As I learned to communicate emotionally with my wife, I found it especially helpful to pay attention to her emotional words and gestures because they most clearly revealed her heart to me. In the same way, as we pray the Psalms, a special interest of ours will be to look for words and phrases in which God reveals his emotions to us.

The Reality and Richness of the Psalms:

"The Psalms…help us see God—God not as we wish or hope him to be but as he actually reveals himself. The descriptions of God in the Psalter are rich beyond human invention. He is more holy, more wise, more fearsome, more tender and loving than we would ever imagine him to be. The psalms fire our imaginations into new realms yet guide them toward the God who actually exists. This brings a reality to our prayer lives that nothing else can." [22]—Timothy and Kathy Keller

For instance, in Psalm 5:5 the writer speaks to the Lord saying, "The arrogant cannot stand in your presence. You hate all who do wrong." *Hate* is a strong word, and even more so when it reveals the heart of God. As we reflect and meditate on this verse, we might be shocked to discover that God is a God who *hates*. He is an emotional being, which is what a personal relationship with God is all about. God shares with us his deep emotions, our spirits are attuned and connected, and our friendship with and love for God matures. We develop a stronger attachment bond with God. Our personal relationship with God deepens.

Superficial, head-to-head dialogue between two humans is just small talk, a surface exchange of information that cannot foster deep interpersonal connections. It's wading in kiddie-pool shallows relationally, whereas emotional sharing is swimming in the deep end of closeness.

When humans share their emotions with one another, it's called intimacy. But when humans and God share heart-to-heart, that's called prayer. According to rabbi Nosson Scherman,

> The Talmud defines man as "the creature that prays." Furthermore, the Talmud teaches that the *nephesh*, the life-sustaining soul, is synonymous with prayer…Prayer, then, is not a list of requests. It is an introspective process, a clarifying, refining process of discovering what one is, what he should be, and how to achieve that transformation. Indeed, the commandment to pray is expressed by the Torah as a service of the heart, not of the mouth. [23]

Lest I be misunderstood, I am not advocating that we exclude reason or facts from prayer. Instead, I'm suggesting that logic and data alone are insufficient in prayer. If we interact with God only cerebrally, we will fail to emotionally connect with God, which is the heart of love and friendship. Prayer is communicating with God not just our thoughts but also our feelings.

In the world of evangelical Christianity, however, the stress has been on knowledge over feelings. Best-selling books emphasize *Knowing God* and *Powerful Prayers*. (I strongly dislike the term "powerful prayers." Prayers themselves are never powerful—only God is.)

In today's Christian ethos, it is easy to misconstrue knowing God as a mostly rational endeavor, and prayer as a mere informational exchange between people and God. We share prayer requests with one another, add these requests to our prayer lists, and then dutifully recite those lists to God daily. For me, this was often a fairly dispassionate exercise. After prayer, I felt pleased to have done my duty before God, but I didn't feel closer to God.

This is why I thank God for the Psalms, which reveal prayer as *primarily* an emotional endeavor. Without the Psalms, prayer can get pretty theoretical; but in the Psalms, prayer is more fervent and passionate than it is accurate. Yes, you heard me correctly—at times the psalmists get so emotionally carried away that they exaggerate the facts. Sometimes the psalmists even pray to God for things that are doctrinally and morally questionable (at times, even wrong—Psalm 137:9).

If this bothers you, dear reader, consider your human relationships. Don't we often express emotions with exaggerations in order to get across the depth of our feelings? "I was so angry I could have throttled him," or "I'm so sad that sometimes I feel like ending it all." And let us not forget that we do this with our positive emotions also: "I have finally found the right man for me—he's just perfect." Here's one I've heard many times: "I'm so happy to have found this church, and you're just the pastor I've been looking for."

So we speak in normal, close relationships with emotive power and hyperbole. Yet with God, we suddenly get stiff and formal in prayer. Of course, no one is more guilty of this than we pastors. We adopt a "pulpit prayer voice" that is unlike our normal speech, and use words and phrases we would never use with our spouses or friends. To be brutally honest, sometimes our pastoral prayers are more like extensions of our sermons than real conversations with God, all done under the guise of prayer. I know how easy it is to fall into this trap.

So I thank God for the Psalms, the book in the Bible that is designed to teach us how to pray. As theologian and Holocaust martyr Dietrich Bonhoeffer wrote, "There is in the Holy Scriptures a book which is distinguished from all other books of the Bible by the fact that it contains only prayers. The book is the Psalms." [24] In a similar vein, Eugene Peterson noted, "If we wish to develop in the life of faith, to mature in our humanity, and to glorify God with our entire heart, mind, soul, and strength, the Psalms are necessary. They are God's gift to train us in prayer." [25]

A Crash Course on Emotions

In addition, the Psalms can increase our emotional awareness, vocabulary, and inventory. In the Psalms we meet a vast array of emotions, a veritable cornucopia of feelings. As we open the Psalms, we walk into a storehouse chock-full of sentiments, a library of passions just waiting for us on each and every shelf.

Adding to Our Library of Emotions:

Atheist blogger turned devoted Catholic Leah Libresco writes about this benefit of praying the Psalms: "The psalms and the strong, varied emotions they express are a kind of training for me. I get to encounter, pray for, and try to understand people experiencing unfamiliar needs, joys, and despairs. These textual experiences help me expand my library of sentiments. Having an archetypal example or handle for a particular category of feeling can make it easier to recognize and respond to this genre of feeling in my day-to-day life." [26]

And we notice this right from the get-go until the finish. This is not an overstatement: the Psalms not only begin and end with emotional verses, but even more, the very first word and the very last word are emotionally charged. "Blessed" in Psalm 1:1 can also be translated "happy," as we will discuss in the next chapter. And "Praise the Lord" in Psalm 150:6 is "Hallelu-Yah," which, in Hebrew, is a compound word expressing overflowing gratitude and celebration. These two verses and two emotional words act as brackets on the whole, which is the ancient Hebrew method of emphasis akin to our use of highlighters or bold fonts. From beginning to end, the Psalms emote.

So let's turn to Psalm 1, which Ellen T. Charry, professor at Princeton Seminary, says "stands as the fiery gateway to the Psalter." [27] Let us open this emotionally charged doorway and step into our prayer adventure through the Psalms, which will strengthen our closest relationships, integrate our emotional and cognitive lives, and launch us on a journey toward deeper attachment with God.

2

Does God Care About Emotions?

Learning to Identify and Value Our Feelings

———————— ✿ ————————

"Blessed is he who expects nothing, for he shall
enjoy everything."[1]—St. Francis of Assisi

Happy are those
   who do not follow the advice of the wicked,
or take the path that sinners tread,
   or sit in the seat of scoffers;
but their delight is in the law of the LORD,
   and on his law they meditate day and night.
               (Psalm 1:1-2 NRSV)

Can you believe it? The very first word in the Psalms is an emotional word: *happy*. Plus, the second verse follows with another emotionally upbeat word: *delight*.

Could God's message to us really be that he desires his people to be delightfully happy? This sounds more like Disneyland than church. Let's be real: if you were given a choice between going to Disneyland (which markets itself as "The Happiest Place on Earth") or attending church, which would bring more of a smile to your face?

Unhappy Christians

Maybe that's one of our problems. Christianity today—in America at least—is perceived as an unhappy religion, the pews of its churches filled with sour-faced Christians.

Oliver Wendell Holmes Jr., who served for thirty years as a Supreme Court justice, said, "I might have entered the ministry if certain clergymen I knew had not looked and acted so much like undertakers." [2] Robert Louis Stevenson wrote in his diary, "I have been to church today and I am not depressed," [3] as if that were a remarkable fact.

Sadly, still today there is some truth in their statements. The church in America is a mixture of Catholic and Anglican liturgical formalism, Presbyterian and Reformed intellectualism, and Baptist and Independent non-emotionalism. We are a melting pot—of dispassionate stuffiness. Sure, there are other denominations that are more expressive with their emotions, but their impact is a ripple in our sea of ecclesial impassiveness. Our culture views the church much like the mother who was sitting with her children alongside her at church. As kids are wont to do, they found something to be funny and began giggling. The mother quickly scolded them, "Stop laughing—you're in church, for Christ's sake!"

This mother's comment is ironic because Jesus was, by all counts, a *joyful* man. The sinners and tax collectors were known to enjoy hanging out with him (Matthew 11:19), and his parables are full of ironic comedy. Because of this, my favorite depiction of Jesus is from the *Visual Bible: Matthew*, in which actor Bruce Marchiano portrays a laughing, happy Jesus. Some members of our church call it "The Smiling Jesus Movie." I think that's great theology.

In Jesus, God came to earth smiling in order to give humans something to smile about—forever. He wasn't just happy; his mission was to build a kingdom of righteousness, peace, and joy (Romans 14:17)—a happy kingdom. He gave instructions on how to be happy, which are known as the Beatitudes "Happy are the…" Matthew

5:3-12, Phillips), and made astonishing promises to his followers about joy. Among these powerful promises are: "I have told you this so that my joy may be in you and that your joy may be complete" (John 15:11), and "Ask and you will receive, and your joy will be complete" (John 16:24). He even prayed to the Father, "I say these things...so that they may have the full measure of my joy within them" (John 17:13).

(As an important side issue, over the years I have heard various pastors try to distinguish between happiness and joy, as if one were temporary and the other longer lasting. In fact, I made this distinction myself until I investigated the biblical terms more closely. As a result, I have written elsewhere[4] that this view is biblically questionable, historically dubious, and etymologically unsound, so in this book I will use *happiness* and *joy* as basically interchangeable.)

Sadly, today's church seems to have less than a full measure of Jesus' joy. Maybe we have not only declawed the Lion of Judah, but we have sedated both our Savior and his bride: neither result is very emotionally vibrant. As scholar Elton Trueblood wrote in *The Humor of Jesus*, "A misguided piety has made us fear that acceptance of His obvious wit and humor would somehow be mildly blasphemous or sacrilegious."[5] What a calamitous turn we have taken from the faith Jesus founded. As a result, most people today search incessantly for happiness in all the wrong places and invariably come up short. We are still experiencing what Henry David Thoreau observed, "The mass of men lead lives of quiet desperation."[6]

But happiness is important. Without it marriages die, physical health deteriorates, and churches misrepresent Christ. The happiness of God that Psalm 1:1 introduces is a foretaste of the happiness revolution that Jesus incarnated. As the *Theological Dictionary of the New Testament* points out, happiness was only for the elites in the Greek and Roman world.[7] In contrast, Jesus' joyous revolution was for everyone, including the lowest of the low. His revolution began a return journey to the idyllic happiness of Eden and will come to full fruition in heaven, which will be like a joyous, happy wedding (Revelation 19:7-9).

Happiness is a big deal to me, so much so that I wrote a whole chapter on "Making Happiness a Habit" in my book, *Praying the Promises of Jesus.* [8] I agree fully with Dennis Prager, who calls happiness "a moral imperative" in his book *Happiness Is a Serious Problem.* [9] Furthermore, I even believe that happiness and joy are clues to the very existence of God—they are rooted in God's nature. [10] Happiness is an important theological and practical issue.

I'm thrilled that the Psalms begin on the emotional tone of happiness, because many of the other Psalms get quite sad, angry, and even depressed. The happy beginning reminds us that though this world is a temporary vale of sorrow, such was neither God's original plan nor ultimate intention. Creation began with singing and joy (Job 38:7), and the new heavens and new earth someday will be rid of sorrow and pain (Revelation 21:4).

To put this bluntly, many people settle for unhappiness, whereas God designed and destined them for joy. Praying Psalm 1 can help us recover God's original intention.

Philip Yancey on the Psalms:

"As the book of Psalms demonstrates so well, prayer does not mean retreating away from life, but rather bringing the stuff of our world—the rhythms of nature, harassing problems, disturbed emotions, personality conflicts—before God, then asking for a new perspective and new energy to take back to that world...Ordinary life prompts many of the psalmists' compositions: a view of stars, sheep on a hillside, family problems, wars and rumors of wars, depression or an emotional high. Read straight through the psalms and you will rail against God, praise God for his faithfulness, wish yourself dead, exult in the beauties of nature, bargain for a better life, and spit curses against your enemies. Psalms keeps me honest by furnishing words to prayers I would not pray apart from their prompting." [11]—Philip Yancey

Blessed or Happy?

Unfortunately, translations of the Bible tend to mask references to happiness with religious sounding words like *blessed* and *rejoice*. Thus, in many Bibles Psalm 1:1 reads, "Blessed is the man who…" just as the Beatitudes likewise sound church-lady approved, "Blessed are the poor in spirit…" In spite of this, the Psalms break forth with a rainbow of happiness-laden words, including *delight, enthrall, dance, glad, happy, joy, jubilant, laugh, pleasant, praise, rejoice*, and *wonder*. At the very least, we believers would be wise to ask, "Are these descriptive of my Christian experience?"

Old habits, however, die hard, and some readers may doubt whether *happy* is a correct translation of the Hebrew *asherey* in Psalm 1:1. The short answer is yes. (If you need the technical facts, they are contained in the endnotes. [12]) For our purposes, it is enough to note that *asherey* is often translated *happy* in the New International Version:

> "Then Leah said, 'How happy (*asherey*) I am! The women will call me happy (*asherey*).' So she named him Asher" (Genesis 30:13).

Her son's name, "Asher," is clearly from the same Hebrew root and means "happy one." If anyone reading this book is considering having kids, I thoroughly recommend this as a name.

> "How happy (*asherey*) your people must be! How happy (*asherey*) your officials, who continually stand before you and hear your wisdom!" (1 Kings 10:8; 2 Chronicles 9:7).

He says to himself, "Nothing will shake me;
   I'll always be happy (*asherey*) and never have trouble."
                           (Psalm 10:6 NIV, 1984)

Daughter Babylon, doomed to destruction,
   happy (*asherey*) is the one who repays you
   according to what you have done to us.
Happy (*asherey*) is the one who seizes your infants
   and dashes them against the rocks.
                            (Psalm 137:8-9)

As these last two verses illustrate, *asherey* is such an emotional word that it is even *inappropriate* at times to translate it *blessed*. (Also, if these verses bother you—and they should!—we will discuss them in chapter 5).

What If the Psalms Were Titled "Happiness"?

As first-year Old Testament students learn, the books of the Hebrew Bible often have quite different titles from those in our English Bibles. In the Torah (Pentateuch), the titles are the first word or words from the text. Occasionally the English and Hebrew titles match up, such as Genesis and *Bereshith*, which means, "In the beginning." Often, they do not. One example is the Hebrew title of Numbers, *Bamidbar*, meaning "In the Wilderness." I've always considered Numbers (which was adopted from the Latin Bible) to be an unfortunate title for English readers. Numbers is a title only accountants or engineers could find appealing, whereas who hasn't gone through a time of wandering "in the wilderness"? Maybe more people would be drawn to read Numbers if it were titled "In the Wilderness."

In a similar vein, the Hebrew title for the book of Psalms is *Tehillum*, meaning "Songs of Praise." Obviously, the title doesn't fit some of the Psalms, such as the extreme Laments (e.g., Psalm 88). But what if the title of the book were based on its first word: *Happy*? And to stretch this idea a bit further, how about *Emotions*? After all, the

Psalms are crammed full of all sorts of emotions, both positive and negative, and praise is just one of them.

In fact, the number of emotional words used in the Psalms is staggering. At least 3100 words[13] carry emotional weight in the Psalms (see appendix 2), and these are contained within only 2461 verses, which calculates to about 1.25 emotional words per verse and 20 per Psalm on average (and even more when we add emotional phrases). When we pray through the Psalms, we pray about emotions.

Emotions are everywhere in the Psalms, just as they are in our daily lives. One author calls them "a constant emotional hum" in our minds.[14] They are sometimes spoken, but most often are communicated nonverbally. As Freud said, "Mortals can keep no secrets. If their lips are silent, they gossip with their fingertips; betrayal forces its way through every pore."[15] To put this positively, we are such emotional beings that we are always feeling something, even if we are unconscious of it. But our bodies know what our minds don't want to face, so we express our emotions constantly through our actions, expressions, and even bodily functions (such as heartbeat or perspiration).

As I pray the Psalms, it is not rare that I feel like suddenly I've stepped onto a roller coaster. They begin climbing upward with happiness and laughter, and then crash down with anger and terror and fear—and that's just in the first two Psalms. From then on, attending to the emotions of the Psalms is an adventure. Up and down, side to side, with several surprising twists and reverses thrown in. We never can anticipate what emotion will come next—sort of like real life. Joyful one moment and sorrowful the next. Content then upset. Loving then hating. Often even two opposite emotions at the same time. Don't try to read the Psalms with your hands in the air or you will be thrown from the car. It's a wild ride through the emotional side of life.

After it dawned on me that the Psalms are drenched with emotions, I also realized that by studying the Psalms I could learn about a huge range of emotions and vastly increase my emotional vocabulary and range. From *abandonment* to *zeal*, I was introduced to a plethora of emotional words.

But my real need wasn't just to learn emotional words in a clinical or philosophical sense. I needed to learn to *feel* them. Most of all, I needed to learn how to feel in my relationships with God and my wife. My wife needed my heart, not just my head. Did God desire the same? It was beginning to dawn on me that the answer to that question is yes.

Belief Is a Matter of the Heart:

As Kathleen Norris points out in her insightful *Amazing Grace: A Vocabulary of Faith*: "I find it sad to consider that belief has become a scary word, because at its Greek root, 'to believe' simply means 'to give one's heart to.' Thus, if we can determine what it is we give our heart to, then we will know what it is we believe."[16]

To this philosopher in recovery, her insight delighted my soul. Too often knowledge is seen as merely cognitive, but philosophers know that our beliefs are built on many intuitive assumptions. These can be called tacit knowledge or properly basic beliefs, but either way they fly beneath the radar of logical proofs. As French philosopher and Christian Blaise Pascal wrote, "The heart has its reasons, the mind knows not of."[17]

I would only add to Norris's comment that in addition to finding our deepest beliefs within our hearts, we also tend to find our hearts when we discover what we give them to. By investigating what we are passionate about, we find our passions, that is, our emotions.

Beginning to Pray the Psalms Emotionally

As we approach God through Psalm 1, we begin by reading the Psalm as a prayer, and at the same time circling or highlighting the emotional words or phrases. Read/pray Psalm 1 (printed below) and highlight anything that strikes you as emotional. (I encourage you to also do this in your own Bible, which will become a spiritual/emotional journal as you pray the Psalms.)

Don't forget as you pray the Psalm, to don your thespian voice as if you were an actor in a play. Read with passion, inflection, and emotion. Let your body get into it; gesture with your posture, your hands, and your face. Our bodies sometimes are more emotionally aware than our minds. As you read aloud with physical passion, you will notice emotive elements that you missed before. Circle any of the additional words or phrases that have an emotional sound or edge to them. As I did this, I circled words like "wicked," "not stand," and "watches over."

So here we go: Read and pray Psalm 1, circling the emotions as you pray.

> Happy are those
>   who do not follow the advice of the wicked,
> or take the path that sinners tread,
>   or sit in the seat of scoffers;
> but their delight is in the law of the LORD,
>   and on his law they meditate day and night.
> They are like trees
>   planted by streams of water,
> which yield their fruit in its season,
>   and their leaves do not wither.
> In all that they do, they prosper.
> The wicked are not so,
>   but are like chaff that the wind drives away.

> Therefore the wicked will not stand in the judgment,
> nor sinners in the congregation of the righteous;
> for the LORD watches over the way of the righteous,
> but the way of the wicked will perish.
>
> (Psalm 1:1-6 NRSV)

How many words or phrases did you circle? Write your total here: _____.

My list totaled nineteen. If yours is less than that, don't be discouraged; this takes practice. Here's my list, verse by verse, for your comparison:

1: happy
   wicked (four times)
   sinners (two times)
   scoffers

2: delight
   meditate

3: planted
   streams[18]
   fruitful
   not wither
   prosper

4: chaff

5: not stand

6: watches over
   perish

Next, prayerfully reflect on each of the emotional words that you circled and add comments next to any words that relate to your daily life or to the lives of those you love.

Last, weave the emotional words and comments into a prayer to your heavenly Father, who longs to connect and attune with you on an emotional level. (Examples of this procedure can be found in appendix 1.)

As I began praying in verse 1, I paused on the first emotional word *happy*. Honestly, I didn't get too far beyond that.

There is just so much to talk with God about when we pray about our happiness or lack thereof. That's the first point on God's prayer agenda for us today. It's fine to read an emotion and join in with it right away, and it is also perfectly acceptable to read an emotion and acknowledge that that's just not where we happen to be at this moment in our lives.

For instance, we can modify the first words of Psalm 1, "Happy are those," to "Happy am I," and take a few moments to list the different sources of our happiness. In my case, as I prayed this Psalm today, I said:

> *Lord, I'm so happy with the life you have given me: I have a*
> *great wife, terrific kids, loving parents, and devoted friends.*
> *You have allowed me to serve in ministry for over thirty*
> *years, and I thoroughly enjoy the privilege of studying and*
> *teaching your Word. You have provided enough money*
> *so we seldom worry about finances and a pleasant home*
> *to call our own. Plus, though my hair has thinned and*
> *turned gray, I still am blessed with good physical health.*

Or you may currently be in an unhappy phase of life—I certainly have had several. In high school my best friend's mom suggested that he not associate with me since I usually seemed unhappy to her. I'm thankful he didn't act on her suggestion. During those months, I could have prayed:

> *Lord, to be honest, I'm not very happy in my life right now.*
> *School and sports are very demanding, and I'm feeling*

*stressed and overworked. Plus, I feel lonely a lot. I'm just
not happy—even you said it's not good for a man to be
alone.*

You get the picture, I'm sure. Now it's your turn. Fill in the blanks
as you see fit.

Lord, I'm so happy with the life you have given me:

_____

_____

_____

Or you may prefer to pray,

Lord, to be honest, I'm not very happy in my life right now:

_____

_____

_____

In either case, the Scriptures become a springboard from which
we can pray about a wide range of topics—most of them close to our
hearts. Since the Psalms are real prayers written by real people, there is
the ring of authenticity to them. Because of this, the psalmists' reflections often give us insight to the sources of our problems and possible remedies as well. It would not surprise me if the source of much
of our unhappiness comes from the same source that the author of
Psalm 1 identifies. In his opinion, what tended to cause unhappiness?
Let's turn to that now.

Psalm 1 and the Most Common Source of Our Unhappiness

As we pray our way through Psalm 1:1, we quickly encounter what the psalmist apparently believed was the cause of much human unhappiness.

> Happy are those
>> who do not follow the advice of the wicked,
> or take the path that sinners tread,
>> or sit in the seat of scoffers.
>> (Psalm 1:1 NRSV)

This is real stuff and sounds to me like complaints I have heard from church members: the grumbles of someone who has listened to the advice of untrustworthy financial advisors and lost money, the sorrow of a person who associated with someone of loose morals and ended up having an affair, or the shame one feels who has been wounded by the cutting sarcasm of others. If we pause to consider what led the psalmist to pray these words to God, we will uncover that each stanza is filled with tremendous emotional weight.

In a nutshell, the psalmist seems to have intimate experience with hanging out with the wrong people, or at least he may have allowed the wrong crowd to influence his thinking. After all, why would he write these very stanzas unless he had firsthand knowledge that bad people can really make one miserable?

(There is another option: maybe someone he loved fell into the bad-company trap, and he is reflecting on her experience. But that still is very close to home. And this gives us yet another way to pray the Psalms: if a Psalm doesn't apply to us, it may apply to someone we care about. We can turn that Psalm into a moment of intercession for those we love.)

The old adage says, "Bad company corrupts good morals." The psalmist is expressing a similar truth, one that most of us have to learn through the school of hard knocks: "Bad company corrupts lasting happiness."

This is a foundational life-truth, which surprisingly escapes many intelligent people. Other people are a primary source of the majority of our happiness as well as unhappiness, and the difference is whom we choose to befriend and share life with. The right people bring gladness, the wrong bring sadness. It really is that simple.

Recently I met with a newly engaged man who didn't seem too happy about it. As we talked, he confided that his fiancée often is domineering, and he fears that she always has to get her own way. This will be his second marriage, and as we talked he flippantly revealed that his ex-wife was also a take-charge person. It wasn't rocket science for me to ask, "In the home you were raised in, who called the shots?" You guessed it—his mom. I asked, "Do you want to have a marriage like your parents? Do you think that will make you happy?"

His instant answer, "No way!"

Every once in a while, God sets up a slam-dunk situation for pastors. There was no way I could miss this one, because this man had actually *tattooed it across his chest* and had showed me his new tattoo with pride (I kid you not). The tattoo read, "Strength!" Indeed, he was a strong man physically, but I could see that he was emotionally weak.

I said, "Here's what I suggest: go to a Christian counselor and find out why you are attracted to women who take charge even though that makes you miserable. And learn how to grow into an emotionally strong man who can hold his own in relationships. God might have led you to get that tattoo, because it's right over your heart. You just have to figure out how to move it from the outside to the inside. Become the man inside that is tattooed on your chest outside!"

Bad Friendships Bring Unhappiness—Bad Marriages Multiply It

As a pastor, I am often shocked at the reasons people choose to marry. Frequently they are quite superficial, and after a few months or years of marriage, the couple doesn't even like each other. The number one reason for this is sex before marriage. Of course, our culture counsels the opposite, claiming that sex before marriage allows a couple to try out the relationship (the principles of consumerism have eclipsed the theology of relationships). In my opinion, the truth is the exact opposite: sex before marriage will *prevent* a couple from truly trying out the relationship. This is because premarital sex is like a switch that shuts off the brain, an eclipse that hides almost everything else from view. [19]

I learned this several years ago from a couple named Brad and Teresa, who asked me to marry them. I asked, "Why do you want a Christian pastor to do your ceremony?"

"We are both Christians, and we want a Christian marriage," they said. "We want God to bless our marriage."

"Okay, then are you approaching this in a Christian way, which is purity before marriage? Or are you saying, 'God, we want you to bless us after marriage, but before the ceremony we will do what we think is best, thank you very much.'"

They sheepishly admitted they had not been pure and felt guilty about it.

So I told them, "Okay, I will consider performing your marriage ceremony, but first you have to commit to one month with no sex, and that means nothing beyond some light kisses. I know it will be hard, but if you do that, we can meet again and discuss the wedding ceremony."

Brad and Teresa agreed, and before the month was over, they called off the wedding. Without sex, they found they had nothing in common. In fact, things that bothered them about one another bubbled to the surface. In the end, they decided they didn't even like each other.

The story has a happy ending. In time they both found others to date, and this time kept their relationships sexually pure before marriage. I performed both weddings, and the two couples were even friends afterward. And for quite some time, in various social settings, one would pull me to the side and say, "Thank you, thank you, Rick. I almost married the wrong person!"

This story is merely an example of how easy it is to choose friends

for the wrong reasons and compromise our values. We all do this—
and it is a destroyer of happiness and an enemy of our emotions.

What Constitutes "Bad Company"

So let's be honest again: Are the friends in your life bringing you
up or down? Have you sought out friendships with mature, responsible people? Do you know qualities to look for in choosing friends—
and most important, a life mate? A good start is right here in Psalm 1:1:

> Happy are those
>> who do not follow the advice of the wicked,
> or take the path that sinners tread,
>> or sit in the seat of scoffers.
>>> (Psalm 1:1 NRSV)

There is so much here that I barely know where to start. How
about we begin with the word *wicked*?

Take a moment to pray this over and over: *"Do not follow the
advice of the wicked, do not follow the advice of the wicked, do not follow the advice of the wicked."* Then ask God to reveal to you whether
there are wicked people in your life that you are following in some
manner. Dwell on this in prayer for a moment or two, and write any
names that come to mind in the margin of your Bible.

"Do not follow the advice of the wicked" is a bold pronouncement:
evil exists, and some people are actually malevolent. This is not a metaphor or hyperbole. Some people are evil, though our culture recoils
at such a judgment. When Ronald Reagan called the Soviet Union
the "evil empire" and George W. Bush labeled Iran, Iraq, and North
Korea the "axis of evil," they were vilified by the secular press. After
all, the secular mindset assumes that if the supernatural does not exist,
then nothing can truly be evil. As God-fearers of many different reli-
gions know, nothing could be further from the truth.

If you happen to doubt the existence of evil, I suggest you read M.
Scott Peck's book, *People of the Lie*. Dr. Peck was a secular psychiatrist

and the author of *The Road Less Traveled*, the publishing phenomenon that ruled the best-seller lists for ten years. He was not a Christian, but was interested in the connection between health, psychology, and spirituality. After *The Road Less Traveled* was published, he encountered some clients who did not fit within his secular understanding. His experience of counseling truly hurtful, cruel people caused Peck to acknowledge the existence of real evil, which in turn led to his conversion to Christianity. Peck discovered what the psalmist also learned: wickedness is real.

I am thankful for the psalmist's frank and upfront warning: evil people exist, and if we want to mess up our happiness, we merely need to open our lives just a bit to their influence. We don't even need to know them personally; just following their advice—or patterning our life, speech, fashions, and finances after them—is enough. The consequence is that our happiness is in jeopardy.

If you are hung up on my "fashions" reference, here are two examples of what I'm talking about: "Gang-chic" and "Hell's Angels look-alikes." How tragic that so many people today follow the patterns set by doers of wickedness.

Here's one more example: horror, zombie, and vampire TV shows and movies. If I haven't offended you yet, this may do it (our church calls me an equal-opportunity offender). This is an oddity of our culture that just boggles my mind. Why would anyone want to let such evil images and behaviors into their minds? Why wickedness as entertainment?

Well, let me answer my own question. There are at least two reasons people are tempted to indulge in this type of material. First, as our culture has become more and more secular, belief in the supernatural (God, angels, demons) has been ridiculed and removed from the reigning worldview. But that didn't make all things supernatural cease to exist. And neither did it fill the need that all humans, beings created for relationship with God, have for the supernatural in their lives. Since people today will not acknowledge the existence of the supernatural, their need sublimates and reappears in their attraction to horror movies, books, and games. E. Michael Jones, in his aptly titled *Monsters from the Id*, chronicles this very phenomenon. [20]

Sometimes the very images of our secular sublimations belie biblical truths. Zombies, for instance, reveal the foundational, tacitly known theological truth—implanted by God in every human heart—that the dead will indeed come back to life on the day of judgment. This is interesting in an awful way: our culture's denial of life after death has resurfaced (should I say resurrected?) in a morbid fascination with enlivened dead bodies. I'll bet the writers and producers of zombie movies and TV shows have no clue that they are expressing deeply spiritual truths about the eternal future of those who reject the gospel.

Second, I believe the current interest in the horror genre is evidence of a diabolical stronghold and scheme. As the apostle Paul assured us, "The weapons we fight with are not the weapons of the world. On the contrary, they have divine power to demolish strongholds" (2 Corinthians 10:4), and "We are not unaware of [Satan's] schemes" (2 Corinthians 2:11). In short, horror is horrible stuff. Stay away from it, don't even get near it, and above all keep it out of your head and heart. It is opening one's mind to the counsel of the wicked.

In the next phrase in Psalm 1:1, the psalmist also cautions us about those closer to home: "or take the path that sinners tread." Some of the people that "tread" near us are those who walk in our social circles, work at our offices, live in our neighborhoods, or go to our schools. The psalmist calls these people "sinners," another word that is very out-of-vogue today. Sinners are not given over to evil like the wicked, but they have opened the door to wickedness and in some manner are living lives opposed to God's original intention. They probably don't see themselves as sinners, for their hearts are calloused and thickened against righteousness.

Lest we get overly judgmental, we must remember that, according to the Bible, we all are sinners and "there is no one righteous, not even one" (Romans 3:10). So how can we avoid "taking the path that sinners tread"?

First, let's get straight that we cannot avoid all sinners, nor should we. We are called to love others, even our enemies, and share our faith in a winsome way. We are to be salt and light in a bland and dark world. Jesus certainly was considered a friend by many sinners (Mark 2:15).

Nonetheless, our happiness is still influenced by those we choose to be our closest friends, and it is wise to walk with those who will raise the spiritual bar in our lives. In sports, athletes improve when they compete against those who are better. It's the same in the emotional arena: happiness is contagious.

The opposite is true as well. Spending too much time with people opposed to God's truths will rub off on us. I've seen this in teenagers who begin to hang around the wrong crowd at school: their speech becomes coarse and their demeanor a tad more rebellious. Little do they know that their path may eventually lead to misery and unhappiness.

Each person is unique, so there are different degrees of sinners. Thus, it is wise to try, in our closer friendships, to congregate with those who truly love and respect God's ways. As Solomon wrote, "Blessed (*asherey!*) is the one who always trembles before God, but whoever hardens their heart falls into trouble" (Proverbs 28:14).

Finally, the psalmist suggests we should not "*sit in the seat of scoffers.*" When this happens, a line has been crossed. Now we aren't just getting advice from afar or walking with questionable company; we've decided to take a seat. We have made ourselves comfortable and apparently intend to stay a while among the scoffers.

Who are scoffers? Those who enjoy scorn, mocking, and sarcasm. I know, I've just described several people in your church—maybe even some of the leaders.

In many churches today, sarcasm is cool. I know I will be ridiculed for this, but I cannot understand how sarcasm became so acceptable in Christian circles. I've heard Christian men belittle and cut each other down, all the while considering it to be a normal, healthy way to interact. I've even heard pastors, in sermons, defend sarcasm as part of benign male bonding rituals.

I beg to differ. The Bible teaches against scoffing and mockery. Two examples among many are, "Above all, you must understand that in the last days scoffers will come, scoffing and following their own evil desires" (2 Peter 3:3), and "Mockers stir up a city, but the wise turn away anger" (Proverbs 29:8). It's just not a wise or edifying way to talk. In fact, the Bible teaches the very opposite: "Do not let any unwholesome talk come out of your mouths, but only what is helpful for building others up according to their needs, that it may benefit those who listen" (Ephesians 4:29). In other words, don't pitch your tent with those who tear others down verbally. You will regret it later.

Putting It All Together

As a quick review, let's again read aloud the prayer of the psalmist,

> Happy are those
>   who do not follow the advice of the wicked,
> or take the path that sinners tread,
>   or sit in the seat of scoffers.
>   (Psalm 1:1 NRSV)

We can pray about the same things. Take a few moments to pause, read, and pray the following:

> *God, I ask you to search my heart, and see if there be any*
>   *wicked way in me (Psalm 139:23-24).*
> *Is there any area of my life that I am following the advice or*
>   *ways of the wicked?*

_____

_____

*Am I associating with any group of people that are a poor
   influence on me?*

_____

_____

*Am I participating in coarse language, scoffing, or sarcasm?
   Am I speaking in ways that are not edifying?*

_____

_____

Amen.

A New Source of Pleasure

After the warning to stay away from happiness-busters, the psalm-ist goes on to describe a new source of pleasure for those who follow God.

> But their delight is in the law of the LORD,
>   and on his law they meditate day and night.
> (Psalm 1:2 NRSV)

When I first read this verse as a teenager, I thought, *Boring!* What could be worse than sitting around reading the Bible, day and night?

I since have discovered that there are lots of behaviors that are worse (I've tried several of them), and though they thrill in the moment, the long-term effect is unhappiness.

Plus, I have learned that meditation is not some ascetic discipline, as it is in Zen Buddhism or Hinduism, which focuses on emptying the mind. Instead, Christian meditation is all about filling our minds with God himself. Like two lovers who cannot stop thinking about one another, biblical meditation is keeping God and his Word on our minds, mulling over his love and truth in our thoughts and even on our lips throughout the day.

As Franz Delitzsch wrote, the Hebrew word for "meditate" is *haggah*, "a deep, dull sound, as if vibrating between within and without, here signifies the quiet soliloquy of one who is searching and thinking." [21] Or in the words of Mitchell Dahood, *haggah* suggests some sort of oral activity. [22] So biblical meditation means this: instead of mumbling to yourself or within your mind, mumble (literally) to God.

Don't believe you can do this? Sure you can—you already do it negatively if you worry. Worry is merely negative meditation; delighting in God and his Word is positive meditation. Like a song that gets stuck in our heads, we can place little bits of Scripture in our minds and think about them over and over.

One of the best ways to do this is to listen to Scripture set to music. Monks do this several times a day as they chant the Psalms. In time, they testify that the words and songs become music in their hearts, filling their days with positive feelings and thoughts.

I have found this to be true also. During an early season in my Christian life, I delighted in different recordings of the Psalms set to music. I played them over and over on my tape deck (it was long ago) and was able to remember them throughout the day. When difficult situations arose in my life, the relevant Scriptures came to mind unbidden, instantly, and helpfully.

Of course, we can also meditate without music. Since we are praying the Psalms, a great practice is to pick a short Scripture from that morning's Psalm for reflection throughout the day. In years past I copied Bible verses onto the back of my business cards, which I never used anyway. Today, the same can be done by texting yourself or taking a screen shot of a verse and making that your phone's wallpaper for the day. Since we tend to look at our phones a lot, this is an especially easy way to keep reminding ourselves to meditate on our daily verse.

And if a verse is especially meaningful or helpful, make it your verse for the week, month, or even year. There is no rush. What's really important is to pay attention to your inner monologues, and replace the harmful ones with helpful words—especially Scripture. Learn to notice your thoughts, particularly when you feel bad. You might be meditating in a self-destructive manner: "I am so stupid," or "God doesn't like me." Exchange these for positive, life-giving content from the Psalms: "I am a tree planted by streams of water," or "The Lord is watching over me in love today."

Since "the word of the Lord endures forever" (1 Peter 1:25), I think it not a stretch to believe that we will have all eternity to delight in and meditate upon Scripture. Imagine your mind never again occupied with worry, fears, or stress. Even more, imagine every human's mind overflowing with God's love and truth, and both of these infusing our relationships and all creation. Minds pure, fulfilled, and happy—just as Adam's and Eve's were before they ate the forbidden fruit. It will be heaven…literally.

Strong and Firmly Planted

Psalm 1 continues with so much wealth and value that this whole book could be devoted to plumbing its depths. Instead, I will let you pray the rest of the Psalm and bask in its insights yourself.

> They are like trees
>   planted by streams of water,

> *Lord, I want to be like this tree…*

_____

_____

> which yield their fruit in its season,
>   and their leaves do not wither.
> In all that they do, they prosper.

Lord, I want to prosper in a way that pleases you...

_____

_____

The wicked are not so,
 but are like chaff that the wind drives away.

Lord, I don't want to be like the unstable wicked...

_____

_____

Therefore the wicked will not stand in the judgment,
 nor sinners in the congregation of the righteous.

*Lord, I especially don't want to fail the test at the final
 judgment...*

_____

_____

For the LORD watches over the way of the righteous,

*Lord, thank you for watching over me, and please also
 watch over these people I care about...*

_____

_____

_____

but the way of the wicked will perish.
                              (Psalm 1:3-6 NRSV)

Lord, when I get jealous of wicked people who seem to have it made in this world, remind me how it will go for them after death, and give me the compassion and courage to share your grace, which is their only hope of avoiding destruction. I pray specifically for these to come to know you...

_____

_____

_____

Amen.

Praying the Psalms in this manner will draw us closer to God and to those we love. Why will this happen? The next two chapters explain how praying the Psalms helps us in tremendous ways relationally, if we look at the Psalms through the lenses of Emotional Intelligence and Emotionally Focused Therapy.

3

Is God an Emotional Being?

The Psalms and Emotional Intelligence

———————— ✿ ————————

"Find the door of your heart, you will discover it is the door to the kingdom of God."—John Chrysostom, archbishop of Constantinople (AD 347–407)

Do you ever get riled up when watching the evening news? If so, prepare yourself (take your blood pressure medicine, if necessary) for the opening stanzas of Psalm 2, because they sound eerily like a poet's angry musings after viewing a six o'clock TV newscast:

> Why do the nations conspire,
>   and the peoples plot in vain?
> The kings of the earth set themselves,
>   and the rulers take counsel together…saying,
> "Let us burst their bonds asunder,
>   and cast their cords from us."
>   (Psalm 2:1-3 NRSV)

Instead of calmly accepting the ways of government leaders, this psalmist wants to "break them with a rod of iron" and "dash them in pieces like a potter's vessel" (Psalm 2:9 NRSV). He is angry, spitting mad at how political leaders have messed up his world.

Prayers for Upset and Fearful People

As we turn to Psalm 2 in praying the Psalms, we encounter an upset and fearful Psalmist. Does this sound familiar? Are there any people or factors in your life that are now causing you to feel distressed or worried? If so, praying this Psalm will be soothing to your soul.

Our method is to begin each day with a simple read-through of a single Psalm, marking all the emotional words and emotionally laden phrases in the passage as we go. This takes some practice because many of us are not accustomed to noticing emotions—either in ourselves or in others. As psychologist Daniel Goleman quips, "Our feelings are often with us, but we are too seldom with them."[1]

Thus, we need to read and pray slowly, trying to feel the psalmist's emotions as if we were reading his poem for the very first time. We pay special attention to affective words and phrases, and *Selah* when appropriate.

Wait a minute, you may be thinking, what is *Selah*?

Surprise: your question contains the answer. *Selah* is a Hebrew word that may have meant "pause" or "rest."[2] Allow me, then, to wait a minute and ask you, dear reader, to reflect on part of a sentence from a previous paragraph: "Many of us are not accustomed to noticing emotions—either in ourselves or in others." Do you tend to do this well or poorly? Do you respond first to what others say or to the feelings that seem to hide behind their words? Cultivating this simple ability has the power to greatly improve almost all relationships.

Give this some thought and prayer before you proceed. Rest, wait,[3] *Selah*.

Let's now return to praying the Psalms and highlight any emotional words and phrases in Psalm 2, reprinted below. Because I needed to improve my skills at noticing the emotions of others, I've found that it helps to imagine that I'm taking my logical glasses off and putting on my emotional lenses.

With your affective specs in place, take a pencil and circle anything in Psalm 2 that might convey feelings or carry either a positive or negative attitude.

> Why do the nations conspire,
>> and the peoples plot in vain?
> The kings of the earth set themselves,
>> and the rulers take counsel together,
>> against the LORD and his anointed, saying,
> "Let us burst their bonds asunder,
>> and cast their cords from us."
> He who sits in the heavens laughs;
>> the LORD has them in derision.
> Then he will speak to them in his wrath,
>> and terrify them in his fury, saying,
> "I have set my king on Zion, my holy hill."
> I will tell of the decree of the LORD:
> He said to me, "You are my son;
>> today I have begotten you.
> Ask of me, and I will make the nations your heritage,
>> and the ends of the earth your possession.
> You shall break them with a rod of iron,
>> and dash them in pieces like a potter's vessel."
> Now therefore, O kings, be wise;
>> be warned, O rulers of the earth.
> Serve the LORD with fear,
>> with trembling kiss his feet,
> or he will be angry, and you will perish in the way;
>> for his wrath is quickly kindled.
> Happy are all who take refuge in him.
>> (Psalm 2:1-12 NRSV)

How many emotions did you count? Write the number here: _____.

If your list is shorter than mine, don't let that bother you. As I said before, this takes practice. Here's my list for your comparison:

    1: conspire, plot in vain

    2: set themselves, take counsel against

    3: burst their bonds asunder, cast their cords

    4: laughs, derision

    5: wrath, terrify, fury

    6: have set

    7: you are my son, I have begotten you

    8: your heritage, your possession

    9: break them, dash them

  10: wise, warned

  11: fear, trembling

  12: kiss his feet, angry, perish, wrath, kindled, happy, refuge

What an astounding assortment of affective words and phrases—almost thirty in a Psalm only twelve verses long!

Feelings Are Valuable Sources of Information:

Shoshana Zuboff, psychologist and professor at Harvard Business School, helps us capture the tremendous value of feelings: "People have to stop thinking of their feelings as irrelevant and messy, and realize they are in fact highly differentiated, nuanced patterns of reaction, knowable sources of information...We will only know what to do by realizing what feels right to us. Attention is our most precious resource. Feelings are our body's version of the situation; everything we want to know about our situation is revealed in our feelings." [4]

In Psalm 2, some words and phrases are clearly emotive, such as "laughs," "wrath," "fear," and "happy." Other words may seem less clear at first, but a designation of them as emotive will make more sense as this book unfolds. For now, let me point out that "refuge" and "you are my son" are examples of *attachment* language, and thus qualify as emotive (see the end of this chapter as well as all of chapter 4). Still others, such as "take counsel against," were not on my initial list. But as I read the passage aloud as if I were an actor reading a script for a play, I imagined other actors whispering together in a conspiratorial tone, and my voice took on a derisive edge—which I later noticed was exactly the same emotion this action evoked from God in verse 4. So I added "take counsel against," because I voiced it with a slightly disgusted tone.

If you still are questioning some of my choices, be assured that this exercise is not a test. Evaluating the emotional content of a word or phrase is often a subjective judgment because it is based on our personal experiences, strengths, weaknesses, and—of course—emotions. Thus, it might be best if, from the start, we agree to disagree about some categorizations. Nonetheless, I encourage you to be open to finding emotional nuances in places where they might have seemed absent to you before. Over time, this will help us stretch and increase our awareness of emotions not only in the Psalms but also in all of life around us.

The incredible number of emotions expressed gives us a hint that the psalmist possessed a high degree of *emotional intelligence*. Since this term may be new to some readers, here is a brief introduction to the concept, after which we will return to praying Psalm 2.

Emotional Intelligence and the Key to Success

Why is it important to increase our awareness of emotions? One answer is that such awareness helps us grow in the emotional skills that are so necessary for success in life and relationships. This is the theory emphasized by *emotional intelligence*, the first *stream of emotional insight* mentioned in an earlier chapter.

One's emotional intelligence is beneficial in every aspect and relationship of one's life. Emotions are everywhere and are highly significant. Indeed, emotions press upon us in the manifold wonders and difficulties of life, as well as reside and reign within. Emotions saturate every aspect of our existence and are crucial to human health, relationships, and success. As Daniel Goleman expressed in his bestseller, *Emotional Intelligence,*

> Much evidence testifies that people who are emotionally adept—who know and manage their own feelings well, and who read and deal effectively with other people's feelings—are at an advantage in any domain of life, whether romance and intimate relationships or picking up the unspoken rules that govern success in organizational politics. [5]

Elsewhere Goleman summed up, "A common core of personal and social abilities has proven to be the key ingredient in people's success: emotional intelligence." [6]

Did you catch that? Emotional intelligence is *the key ingredient* in success. And this applies not just to relational success. In case after case, Goleman documented that high emotional intelligence leads to greater success in corporate leadership, sales and marketing, personal health and wellness, and even research and medical science. For instance, studies reveal that *among scientists,* emotional intelligence is "four times more important than IQ in determining professional success and prestige." [7] Yes, you read that correctly: emotional intelligence is more important than IQ even in the careers of scientists.

Switching fields to executive management, in a study of top executives at fifteen global companies, "Emotional competence made the crucial difference between mediocre leaders and the best. The stars showed significantly greater strengths in a range of emotional competencies...On average, close to 90 percent of their success in leadership was attributable to emotional intelligence." [8]

From the petri dish to the boardroom, enhancing our emotional intelligence pays off. If we want to do better at work, we usually can do so by simply increasing our emotional intelligence.

Of course, emotional intelligence is also important in our inter-personal relationships and extremely so in our marriages, families, and friendships. There emotions rule, for better or worse. As Gole-man put this, "The brightest among us can founder on the shoals of unbridled passions and unruly impulses; people with high IQs can be stunningly poor pilots of their private lives."[9]

It's no surprise that the authors of the Bible figured this out long ago. A robust and balanced emotional life, which psychologists call high emotional intelligence, was described by the apostle Paul as *the fruit of the Spirit*: "Love, joy, peace, forbearance, kindness, goodness, faithfulness, gentleness and self-control" (Galatians 5:22-23a).[10] Truly, "Against such things there is no law" (Galatians 5:23b). And the Psalms, of course, massively display these emotional qualities.

In spite of the obvious value of emotional intelligence, known intuitively throughout human history, it is a rather recent discovery in the social sciences. To put it bluntly, thinking has trumped feeling in science and academia ever since the triumph of rationalism in the Enlightenment. Since then, humans are even defined scientifically as *homo sapiens*—thinking beings. But we are more than thinking beings—we are emotional beings too. In fact, emotions may be the final arbiter in much of our decision-making. Reasons play their part, but the final decision occurs in the emotional (limbic) portion of our brains.[11] (Maybe humans should be renamed *homo affectus!*)

Various psychologists and social scientists first discussed the notions related to emotional intelligence as early as the 1960s. It wasn't until 1990, though, that Peter Salovey and John Meyer defined emotional intelligence as five key emotional competencies: knowing one's emotions, managing emotions, motivating oneself, recognizing emotions in others, and handling relationships.[12]

It was left, then, to Daniel Goleman, a Harvard trained psy-chologist, to expound upon and popularize the concept in 1995 in

Emotional Intelligence. Since that time, his devotion to this topic has made emotional intelligence a household term and has launched a blizzard of academic studies, spawned shelves of related books, and created a cottage industry of corporate seminars and workshops.

What Are Emotions?

In order to better understand and fully pray the emotions in the Psalms, it is helpful to define what an emotion is. It is easy to assume that an emotion is merely a feeling or passion, but the reality is more complex. Many emotions are a mixture of sub-emotions, and they arise not only from an inciting event but also from prior experiences that nuance them. Our past experiences somewhat dictate what emotions we feel in the present. In addition, emotions are not dumb; they are efforts to communicate our inner states; they are "speech acts." An infant not only emotes but also is unconsciously trying to communicate through those emotions—and will continue to do so for a lifetime.

So what is an emotion? Maybe an expert's definition will help us here. Goleman shares both the dictionary definition as well as his own:

> In its most literal sense, the *Oxford English Dictionary* defines *emotion* as "any agitation or disturbance of mind, feeling, passion; any vehement or excited mental state." I take *emotion* to refer to a feeling and its distinctive thoughts, psychological and biological states, and range of propensities to act. There are hundreds of emotions, along with their blends, variations, mutations, and nuances. Indeed, there are more subtleties of emotions than we have words for. [13]

Thankfully, researchers have worked to reduce the number of core emotions to a manageable number (though there is no absolute agreement on the matter). Goleman fetchingly calls these core sentiments "the emotions that can be considered primary—the blue, red, and yellow of feeling from which all blends come." [14] He lists eight primary emotions but helpfully includes many of the related "blends" also:

- *Anger*: fury, outrage, resentment, wrath, exasperation, indignation, vexation, acrimony, animosity, annoyance, irritability, hostility, and, perhaps at the extreme, pathological hatred and violence

- *Sadness*: grief, sorrow, cheerlessness, gloom, melancholy, self-pity, loneliness, dejection, despair, and when pathological, severe depression

- *Fear*: anxiety, apprehension, nervousness, concern, consternation, misgiving, wariness, qualm, edginess, dread, fright, terror; as a psychopathology, phobia and panic

- *Enjoyment*: happiness, joy, relief, contentment, bliss, delight, amusement, pride, sensual pleasure, thrill, rapture, gratification, satisfaction, euphoria, whimsy, ecstasy, and at the far edge, mania

- *Love*: acceptance, friendliness, trust, kindness, affinity, devotion, adoration, infatuation, *agape*

- *Surprise*: shock, astonishment, amazement, wonder

- *Disgust*: contempt, disdain, scorn, abhorrence, aversion, distaste, revulsion

- *Shame*: guilt, embarrassment, chagrin, remorse, humiliation, regret, mortification, contrition [15]

Doesn't that list remind you of the emotions found in the Psalms?

Where Do People Experience Emotions?

"One of the hallmarks of close relationships is emotion, both positive and negative. Where else but in close relationships do people experience such diverse and intense feelings as acceptance, security, love, joy, gratitude, and pride—on the positive side, and frustration, rage, hatred, fear of rejection, humiliation, grinding disappointment, jealousy, grief, and despair—on the negative side."—Psychologists Mario Mikulincer and Phillip R. Shaver[16]

It occurs to me that another answer to their question, "Where else but in close relationships do people experience such diverse and intense feelings…" is *sports*—especially for men. Athletes can laugh, curse, yell, and feel despair, all in the course of a game or match. And spectators can do the same! Sports and other forms of entertainment are the modern, socially approved outlets for emotions. How many wives believe they are married to unemotional men—except when their favorite team is playing on TV?

Praying for People Who Disgust You

With our increased understanding of the value of emotions, it's time to apply this to our understanding of God, others, and even ourselves. Let's return to Psalm 2 and notice *whose* emotional intelligence (EI) is revealed in each verse:

Verses 1-3: conspire, plot	The EI of secular people
Verses 4-6: laughs, derision	The EI of God
Verses 7-9: son, father, refuge	The EI of the psalmist
Verses 10-12a: warned, trembling	The EI of secular people
Verse 12b: angry, wrath	The EI of God
Verse 12c: happy, refuge	The EI of the psalmist

The psalmist begins by talking about the plans, behaviors, and emotions of "nations," "peoples," "kings," and "rulers." These people were foreign leaders whom the psalmist worried about—secular forces and excitable populations who were opposing Israel. The psalmist might have overheard rumors or perhaps was given military reports of enemies who were scheming together to attack the people of God, and therefore God himself. They were "plotting" and "conspiring," establishing hardline positions ("setting themselves"), and "taking counsel together." The psalmist gives us a clear view of the emotional status of the enemy, that is, the emotional intelligence of his foes. In short, they were planning coordinated attacks on Israel, so the psalmist was clearly feeling unsafe.

This is exactly how millions of people feel today as scores of countries deal with terrorism in grand proportions.

I write this chapter in late 2015, about fourteen years after 2997 people were murdered on 9/11, three weeks after 224 were killed aboard a passenger jet on its way from Saudi Arabia to Russia, and just two days after attacks in Paris left over 120 dead. In all three cases, the murderers were Islamic terrorists in planned, coordinated attacks. People across the globe are worried. When will the next barbarous attack happen—and where? Everyone realizes it could be close to home, and a loved one could be a victim.

The two scenarios, both in the time of the psalmist and present-day, are tragically similar. Though separated by almost three millennia, we both have enemies who scheme against us, and we feel powerless to stop them. What can we do? We can join the psalmist in prayer:

> Why do the nations conspire
>   and the peoples plot in vain?

> *Lord, why do nations like _____ and*
>   *_____ conspire against us,*
>   *and why do terrorists scheme to kill us?*
>   *My heart grieves for the innocent people who were*
>   *murdered and for their families who have been stricken*
>   *with sorrow. Why, Lord, why? Why would anyone do such*
>   *a thing?*

*Lord, I pray for these communities who have been schemed
against, and the families who have been torn apart:*

_____

_____

The kings of the earth set themselves,
   and the rulers take counsel together,
   against the LORD and his anointed, saying,

> *Ah, now I understand, Lord. They are rebelling against
> you, and against those of us who have been blessed by you.
> They may not even know this,
> but they are really trying to kill you, God,
> and set up their own idols in your place.*

"Let us burst their bonds asunder,
and cast their cords from us."

> *Lord, in their heart of hearts they are defying you, trying to
> break apart the moral bonds you have set on all humans,
> severing the very cords that restrict in your loving wis-
> dom. Without those boundaries, chaos will ensue, which is
> just what the evil one wants for them and for us. Don't let
> them succeed, Lord!*
> *God, please reveal yourself to them and burst apart the spiri-
> tual strongholds that enslave them! Amen.*

Wow! Suddenly this ancient book of poetry has become very
relevant.

It might be, however, that this Psalm also applies to you or
someone you love in a current, more personal, way. That is, maybe

someone in your life is trying to hurt and destroy you, scheming with others to bring you down. Because of their threats you have been terribly worried and afraid.

Take heart—you are not alone. Problems like this have been going on for thousands of years. But before you respond impulsively, do what the psalmists did: take the matter and your emotions to God in prayer. This time, I challenge you to write out your own prayers in response to each Scripture:

> Why do the nations conspire,
>   and the peoples plot in vain?
>
>> *Lord, people are conspiring against me, and I'm so worried*
>>   *and afraid.*
>> *This makes me feel:*

> The kings of the earth set themselves,
>   and the rulers take counsel together,
>   against the LORD and his anointed, saying,
>
>> *Lord, these people are scheming together against me,*
>>   *and against you:*

> "Let us burst their bonds asunder,
>   and cast their cords from us."

Lord, they are trying to be free of your morals and controls.
What they are doing is just wrong, such as:

_____

_____

Don't let them succeed, Lord! Amen.

The psalmist is clearly angry and yet does not sin (Ephesians 4:26). As C.S. Lewis wrote, "The absence of anger, especially that sort of anger which we call indignation, can, in my opinion, be a most alarming symptom. And the presence of indignation may be a good one." [17]

Our Emotional Father in Heaven

When we feel under such attack, it is very common to emotionally respond, "God, where are you? Why are you allowing this?" So the psalmist turns now to God and—shockingly—first reveals to us God's own feelings about our trouble, that is, reveals to us a bit of the emotional intelligence of God.

> He who sits in the heavens laughs;
>   the LORD has them in derision.
> Then he will speak to them in his wrath
>   and terrify them in his fury, saying,
> "I have set my king on Zion, my holy hill."
>   (Psalm 2:4-6 NRSV)

Like a lightning bolt out of heaven, suddenly we learn a tremendous fact: *God is an emotional being.* God has feelings, an insight that is consistent with the rest of Scripture. For instance, we have long known that God loves and cares for his children. Moreover, the Bible proclaims, "God is love" (1 John 4:8, 16). We know that God "cares" (1 Peter 5:7), "rejoices" (Isaiah 62:5), and "delights" (Micah 7:18). Since Christians have talked for years about having a personal relationship with God, this makes sense. After all, what kind of personal relationship could anyone have with a God of no emotions?

In Psalm 2, God reveals himself to us as one who "laughs" and "derides," as well as one who "terrifies" humans with his "wrath" and "anger." This is not the God presented in most children's Sunday school lessons, nor is it the God heard in typical evangelical seeker-services today. Truth be told, these were not the emotions of God that I emphasized in most of my own sermons. The wrath of God is not a popular topic, except by ardent atheists who claim this is a reason to *disbelieve* in God. A God of love is in; a God of hate is out.

Yet the God revealed in the Bible is a passionate God, one who deeply embodies what appear to us as both positive and negative emotions—coexisting together without conflict. There are about 350 references in the Bible to the "wrath," "anger, " and "fury" of God, and over 250 more concerning the "fear," "trembling," and "dread" of the Lord (which point to the perceived wrath of God[18]). In addition, the Bible openly admits that God feels "sadness," "grief," and "contempt," which bolder translators might have rendered as "disgust."

Anger in God and in Us:

Neil Clark Warren's helpful book *Make Anger Your Ally* points out interesting facts about anger in the Bible: "God is reported as being angry seven hundred times in the Old Testament alone. Jesus was regularly angry in relation to those who opposed him and toward his own disciples as well. Leading figures throughout Biblical history—prophets, kings, and other designated leaders—frequently are described as angry. When Moses, for example, came down from the mountain and found the Israelites forming a golden calf to worship, the Bible says that he threw down the stone tablets which contained the law, and his anger 'waxed hot'...The Bible recognizes anger as a biological given. The very Hebrew words which are translated 'to be angry' literally mean 'to snort' and 'to be hot or passionate.' Anger has a distinctly physical quality about it, and the capacity for anger is present in everyone."[19]

Upon deeper reflection, these negative sounding God-emotions should not surprise us at all. In fact, we should be shocked if God did not feel them. Think about a human who never felt anger, fear, or contempt. Such a person would either be a moral monster, for whom nothing appeared terribly wrong or cruel, or a person suffering from what psychiatrists call *alexthymia,* (from the Greek roots "*a-*" for "not", "*lexis*" for "word," and "*thymos*" for "emotion"[20]), a disability in which a person is unable to feel or express emotions.

Is God unable to feel or express emotions? To assume that God is nonemotional would lead to one of the two problematic conclusions noted above: a wrath-less God would be, like the nonfeeling human, either disabled or a moral monster, which turns the atheist argument on its head. An emotionless God would be a moral monster, so the wrath of God may be a good reason to believe in his existence!

Therefore, we ought to thank God that there are things that peeve and upset him in a world like ours. It's called righteous anger. God is a being who can be moved to anger, fury, and hate as well as love and compassion. As Old Testament scholar Walter Brueggemann asserts, "The true believer hates powerfully and finds a community with Yahweh (the God of Israel) who also hates."[21]

(Warning! Philosophy ahead. If you are not interested in philosophical theology, feel free to skip the next several paragraphs.)

To be fair, some theologians hold an opposite position called *divine impassibility* (or *apatheia*), from the Latin roots meaning "not" (*im-*) and "suffer" (*passio*). The logic that supports this view flows this way:

1. God is all-powerful.

2. If God can feel emotions (grief, for example), that implies that he is changeable due to circumstances.

3. Anything that is changed by another is the less powerful of the two.

4. Statements 2 and 3 lead to: God is less powerful than anything that caused his emotions to change.

5. Conclusion: it cannot be the case that God grieves or has emotions, since statements 1 and 4 are contradictions.

So there is a valid philosophical reason to conclude that God is unfeeling. Since that is the case, why do I hold the opposite view? My answer is the Psalms! God is revealed there (as well as in the rest of the Bible) as a very emotional God, a personal being who loves, cares, and feels.

I think the doctrine of the impassivity of God is rooted in the philosophy of Aristotle rather than in the Bible. Aristotle's famous description of God was "*noesis-noeseos-noesis*," [22] which meant "Thought-thinking-thought." This definition implied, according to many philosophers, that God was not only impassive and aloof, but that he was some sort of heavenly narcissist, contemplating his own contemplations, that is, his own self. He would be the ultimate navel-gazer.

While I believe this is an inaccurate understanding of Aristotle, that is not germane to our discussion. What is relevant is the idea that God, as "Thought-thinking-thought" suggests, is rational rather than emotional. The Psalms, however, clearly teach he is both. In fact, since the Bible rarely mentions God "thinking" (a rare example is Psalm 139:17: "How precious to me are your thoughts, God! How vast is the sum of them!"), but has over a thousand references or allusions to the feelings of God, maybe it would be better to describe God as "Emotion-emoting-emotions." [23]

More precisely, we must hold together both attributes: God is a "feeling-thinking-feeling" God. Both qualities are necessary for true personhood and for meaningful relationships to occur. The God revealed in the Bible is not only omniscient (all-knowing) but also *omni-emotional* (to coin a phrase), and never more so than in the Psalms.

Attuning with God's Vulnerable Display of Emotions

When friends and family members trust us enough to reveal their most heartfelt emotions, it is both an honor to be appreciated and a responsibility to handle delicately. But it is also an opportunity, a chance to draw close, heart-to-heart, on a deep level of interpersonal intimacy. The sharing of authentic, emotional vulnerabilities is what creates deep relational bonds and psychological connections, which are the very stuff that love is made of. When true emotions are shared, an exceptionally valuable gift has been given.

Emotional and Spiritual Rehab:

Christian psychologists Tim Clinton and Joshua Straub, in *God Attachment*, remind us that drawing close to God won't be instant or easy, and there are no quick fixes: "Emotional and spiritual healing is certainly possible, but it happens far more like rehab than the miracle surgery, far more like the slow-turning rheostat bringing light incrementally than a light switch…The metaphor of physical rehab as a description of emotional and psychological healing isn't as sexy or glamorous as the promise of instant healing, but it's a far more accurate description of the real process God takes us through as we address our relationships and learn to connect with him and others." [24]

Their book is built upon a core truth: "We were wounded in relationships, and we are healed in them too." In response I can only say, "Amen and amen!" I also believe the psalmists would reply, if they were here today,

Bless the LORD, O my soul,
　and all that is within me,
　　bless his holy name.
Bless the LORD, O my soul,
　and do not forget all his benefits—
who forgives all your iniquity,
　who heals all your diseases,
who redeems your life from the Pit,
　who crowns you with steadfast love and mercy,
who satisfies you with good as long as you live
　so that your youth is renewed like the eagle's.
(Psalm 103:1-5 NRSV)

So when we come to pray a verse like Psalm 2:5, we have a special opportunity to attune to this astounding display of emotional vulnerability on God's part. When God shares emotionally with us, we have a chance to cherish his gift, cradle it as a fragile treasure, and bond with him on a Spirit-to-spirit level.

The only thing I can compare this to is when each of our three children was born. The doctors gave each newborn first to my wife to hold, which was appropriate since she did all the work. When she gave each of them to me, in turn, those moments were highpoints in my life. Each child was a rare, fragile gift given to her and me from God himself. At the same time, these first newborn minutes were crucial bonding moments for all of us. As I held our infants, I instinctively attuned to their emotions and needs. I was fully alert and attentive, rocking them gently, even singing softly to soothe them— and I rarely sing to anyone. We were all emoting together, emotions-emoting-emotions. Those truly were divine moments.

Not all moments since then have been quite so divine. As kids grow, they emote less and less around their parents, and fall into the false notion that sharing emotions is a sign of weakness. My wife countered this by asking often, "What do you feel about...?" which the kids usually grumbled about. But in the vital moments, she was there for them emotionally, treating their feelings like fragile treasures. I have no doubt those moments contributed strongly to the attachment bonds between Amy and each of our kids.

Unfortunately, I responded poorly when she asked the same of me, 'Rick, what do you feel about...?" I didn't like dealing with my emotions, so I usually avoided the issue. Over time, she gave up asking the question.

But now that the eyes of my heart (Ephesians 1:18) have been opened to the power and value of emotional sharing, we both are asking this question of each other—a lot. And I don't mind it a bit. I now know she is really saying, "I want to connect with you on a deep, intimate level. I want to know what's going on in your heart, not just your head." So I emote, she emotes about my emotions, and we both end up as emotions-emoting-emotions. Trust me, it's a lot better than fighting or feeling distant.

So let's attune with our emotional heavenly Father by praying the Psalms.

> He who sits in the heavens laughs;
>   the LORD has them in derision.

> *God, it's so reassuring to hear that you laugh in the face of*
>   *evil, that it doesn't worry or frighten you. It's also so com-*
>   *forting to know that if you aren't worried, then I needn't*
>   *be either. Therefore, I give you these concerns for you to*
>   *laugh at:*

> _____

> _____

> Then he will speak to them in his wrath
>   and terrify them in his fury, saying,

God, I'm also very thankful for this reminder that some things anger you, and even make you furious. It reminds me that there are real rights and wrongs in this moral universe, because you made it and it reflects your moral qualities.

There are some matters that I'm angry about right now, in my life and in this world. I give them now to you, and I ask you to guide me. Are these matters that make you angry also? If not, please help me let go of them:

"I have set my king on Zion, my holy hill"
(Psalm 2:4-6).

God, as you installed your king in Jerusalem so many years ago, in order to be prepared to defeat those who made you angry, please remind me that the King of kings, Jesus your Son, is also on his throne in heavenly Zion, and I can trust him to defeat evil when you deem best. Help me to remember to trust in the power of the King of kings more than in these evils that anger me so:

Amen!

When Our Emotions Come Out of Hiding

The last few verses of Psalm 2 reveal emotional language of a different type: "son," "begotten," and "take refuge."

These phrases reveal close bonds and feelings of safety and security.

What is fascinating to me is that these intimate feelings emerged out of the emotional sharing between God and the psalmist displayed in the first half of the Psalm. When those in a relationship share their inner emotions—especially vulnerable, potentially embarrassing emotions such as weakness, fear, and worries—deeper bonds are formed and strengthened between them.

This is evidence of what psychologists call *attachment*.

Attachment will be the subject of the next chapter, but there is such a gem here in Psalm 2 that I can't skip over it.

> I will tell of the decree of the LORD:
> He said to me, "You are my son;
>   today I have begotten you."
> (Psalm 2:7 NRSV)

The heart of attachment, especially in the formative stage in the parent-child relationship, is that it establishes a safe place, a foundation in which the child feels secure and from which the child can venture forth to safely investigate the world. As we will see in the next chapter, a child with a secure attachment bond with at least one caregiver—usually one or both parents—is equipped to build healthy relationships for the rest of his or her life. Conversely, children with poor attachment bonds may have a difficult time relationally and emotionally.

Since it all comes down to *secure attachment*, what could be more powerful to a worried and fearful psalmist than to hear, "You are my son...I have begotten you"? It's an extremely robust attachment phrase. It signifies an intimate yet strong relationship, a commitment upon which Israel clearly has the safest of secure havens. God himself is Israel's, and therefore the psalmist's, heavenly Father, his almighty protector. It doesn't get any more fortified than that. [25]

Because of this, the Psalm ends with, "*Happy are all who take refuge in him.*" "Refuge" (mentioned forty-three times in the Psalms) is also a great attachment word, like so many others in the Psalms: "rock" (twenty-eight times), "mighty fortress" (seventeen times), "strong-hold" (ten times), "under his wings" (six times), and "tower" (once). These are fantastic assurances of the psalmist's safe relationship with God, his protected haven that can never be shaken.

Rather than praying them now, let's turn to the next chapter and give Emotionally Focused Therapy and Attachment Theory their full due, during which we can embrace and pray Psalms 3 and 4.

4

Building a Secure Attachment with God

The Psalms and Emotionally Focused Therapy

———————— 🌿 ————————

"Our experience with thousands and thousands of couples
has shown that the one element most often lacking in
Christian marriages is emotional intimacy, and sadly,
many have settled for this heartless state of intimacy—
thinking they'll never find more."[1]—Joe Beam,
founder of *Family Dynamics*

In Psalm 3, we hear emotional pleas that—how can I say this respectfully?—could be the words of a fearful preschooler afraid to go to bed at night. If you are a parent, I'm certain this has happened to you.

You put your child to bed (though he pleads that he doesn't want to go to sleep yet) and insist that he try to sleep. You pray, hug, kiss, and even get him an extra drink of water. ("Please, Daddy, I'm soooo thirsty!") Finally, you turn out the light, exit the room, and close the door.

A few moments later, the lovely silence is pierced by soft cries or even loud screams. You rush into the room only to find your child wide-awake with fear. "Daddy, I'm so afraid. I think there are monsters under my bed…or in the closet…or outside my window. I can't sleep."

What does your child need at this moment? A logical discourse on the nonexistence of monsters? A sarcastic comment such as, "Don't be a baby"? An angry response that it is disobedience to stay awake?

Each of these might be tempting responses in the heat of the moment, but hopefully you recognize that your child doesn't need reasons, ridicule, or retorts. What he needs is *emotional* connection and reassurance. Another hug, kiss, and reminder that you are just in the next room. He needs *emotional* assurances that you are near, attentive, and protective, which are communicated through loving touch, soothing words, and—most of all—physical presence. (This requires great parental wisdom, since it also is possible to overindulge children.) Finally, he will drift off to sleep, knowing that because of who you are, his home is a safe haven.

In light of this common scenario, listen to phrases from the first six verses of Psalm 3 and compare them to our nighttime conversations with our kids.

> *Lord, how many are my foes*
>
>> "Daddy, there are monsters in my room."
>
> *I cry aloud*
>
>> "Waaaah! Daddy, I need you!"
>
> *He answers me*
>
>> "It's okay, son, I'm here. I was just in the next room, ready to help when needed. I won't let any monsters get you."
>
> *I lie down and sleep*
>
>> "Will you leave the door open a bit so I know you can hear me? Yes? Then okay, I'll try to go to sleep again."
>
> *I will not fear*
>
>> "Since you are near, I don't need to be afraid."

Psalm 3 reveals that troubles, fears, and cries aren't experienced only in childhood. Psalm 4 continues along the same lines:

"Answer me when I call to you..."
"Give me relief from my distress..."
"The Lord hears when I call to him..."
"Trust in the Lord" (Psalm 4:1,3,5)

These Psalms, both attributed to King David, show that even normally courageous adults have such feelings at times, and they are notoriously difficult to conquer.

Let's get personal: how often have you lain awake at night, worrying about some monster at the office who is making your life miserable or a financial scenario that you are dreading? When was the last time you couldn't sleep because *really awful thoughts* (I call these RATs) kept gnawing inside your brain? Though you knew doctrinally that God is love and that he has promised to be your helper in times of need, you weren't feeling very reassured or secure.

I've done this all too often—including last night.

I could not sleep because of what happened earlier in the evening. I was invited to a board meeting, but when I arrived, the chairman (who can be a real bully at times) treated me very poorly. He verbally attacked me and falsely maligned my character—in front of a group of people no less (thereby violating Matthew 18:15-20). I defended myself, which only earned me further rude treatment from someone else. I left the meeting feeling alone, hurt, embarrassed, and angry, which are the kind of emotions that make it difficult to sleep.

Feelings like these are common for both adults and children, and we need safe relationships in which we can share our wounded feelings. I was so thankful to have a close heavenly Father with whom I could vent my feelings on the drive away from the meeting, and a secure marriage to welcome me home. We all need reassurance that we are not alone, that strong and capable loved ones are available to help when needed, and—most of all—that these loved ones truly care about us. We all need people with whom we feel close and connected, safe and secure, loved and treasured. Psychologists call this *secure attachment*, which must happen on an emotional level and not merely an intellectual one. Let me put it this way: it's not enough for those you love to know you love them—they must *feel* loved.

What I Discovered Was Missing in My Marriage

As my wife and I began marriage counseling, we bought books and workbooks, including some on the secular counseling approach called Emotionally Focused Therapy (EFT). As I listened to our therapist and read these books, I felt like the apostle Paul: scales fell from my eyes, and I was able to see—on a deeper level than ever before—the importance of emotions in relationships.

That's when I discovered what Amy needed most from me: not rational proof that I loved her but emotional proof. We both needed to feel loved, though at first we didn't realize this. We knew we were missing the mark somehow, and it was through this emotional awareness training that we were able to begin our journey toward a more satisfying marriage.

In a nutshell, I learned that *emotions are the language of love*. Relationships flourish because of emotional sharing and vulnerability, whereas relationships without that wither and die. My wife and kids desperately needed to connect with me emotionally, and not just spend time together playing games, doing chores, or watching TV. They needed me to reveal my inner self to them, which demanded that I find out what was inside me that I had so carefully hidden from others—and myself. And I needed the same from them.

This was hard for me. I had learned somewhere to keep my problems to myself and that sharing worries or fears is a sign of weakness. In addition, I believed that showing my emotions would unnecessarily burden others. So in my marriage I kept quiet about any worries or concerns, thinking I was helping my wife by not sharing my problems with her. Actually, I was starving her spirit—and mine as well.

When the scales fell from my eyes, I began to venture carefully into this new territory. For instance, I came home one day, worried about some financial problems that loomed on our distant horizon. In the past, I would have simply kept that concern bottled up inside, protecting my wife from the worry. This time, I did the opposite. I shared that I was worried, revealing both the details along with my feelings of failure and embarrassment.

Then I asked the really vulnerable question: "How does hearing this stuff make you feel?" I assumed she would say, "Worried and afraid." She shocked me by replying, "I feel closer to you than I have in a long time. I like it when you trust me and open up to me like that."

I said (with fear and trembling), "Doesn't it make you feel less of me as a man?"

Another shocker. She said, "No, it makes me respect and love you more."

It's crazy but true: emotions are the language of love. Don't try to make sense of them—just go with them. And your closest relationships will blossom as if rain, after a long drought, has finally fallen on parched soil.

Emotionally Starving Family Members

Sadly, many marriages and families are in the same boat I was. They are suffering from a long emotional dry spell. As my eyes are more open to the importance of emotional sharing, I see many people who could benefit greatly from learning how to identify and share emotions.

Here's an actual example that is playing out as I write (the names are changed). Ken and Mary have been married fifteen years and have two preteen daughters. Ken is a hardworking, moral, respectable man who is doing his best to provide financially for his wife and children. But Ken is completely unaware that his emotional connections with his wife and girls are withering. Ken apparently thinks that manliness is never admitting struggles, fears, or doubts—even to his wife. She knows he loves her intellectually and volitionally, but there is no emotional closeness between them. She feels unwanted and unloved.

His girls are not granted access to his heart either. He takes them to church and coaches their softball teams, but rarely connects on an emotional level with them. In time, I believe, Ken's emotional absenteeism may create in them a propensity to seek emotional closeness from teenage boys and young men.

I wish I could say to Ken: "Ken, your wife and girls need more of you emotionally. They need you to open up and appropriately share with them your hurts, fears, and dreams. They need to connect with you on an emotional level—often. If you don't, they will unconsciously be driven to seek that elsewhere from other men."

Is it too late for Ken and his family? No, but he has some catch-up work to do. (If you are a friend of mine and wondering if this story is about you—yes it is. All of you.)

In his heart of hearts, I know Ken loves his wife and children and wants his connection with them to be deep and lasting. He just doesn't know how to do that. Neither did I, but I was learning fast. And it brought me a deeper level of intimacy not only with my family and friends, but with God.

Emotionally Healthy Adulthood and Spirituality

Ever since my decision to follow Christ as a high school senior, I have longed for a closer walk with God. So I committed to daily Bible reading and prayer—for a season even praying an hour each day. I attended prayer meetings, prayer concerts, and prayer vigils. I fasted for several days at a time. I earned my doctorate of ministry in spiritual formation and read thousands of pages written by the giants of devotional literature. But throughout that journey, I can't recall ever hearing that what I needed in order to grow closer to God was to learn how to connect with God on an emotional level. Maybe I skipped those pages.

I also wanted to be the best husband, father, and man that I could be. So like many Christian men, I attended men's Bible studies, read books about Christian manhood, and attended Promise Keepers rallies in the 1990s. I went to marriage retreats and marriage confer-ences and read many books on marriage and relationships. For the life of me, though, I can't remember any stress on the importance of emotionally attuning with my wife, kids, or with God.

Because of this, I had a lot to learn about the necessity of emo-tions in relationships when I first heard about Emotionally Focused Therapy (EFT) and the theory behind it. Fortunately, I was already praying and studying the Psalms (which is what I call a coinc-a-God), so as I dug into the history and psychology behind this type of ther-apy, I found it to be absolutely fascinating—and very relevant to the Psalms. The new insights about emotional closeness fit hand-in-glove with my prayer life. I received a double benefit: I grew closer—almost instantly—as I shared emotionally with my wife and with God. EFT told me I needed to connect emotionally with others; the Psalms showed me how to do exactly that.

For example, I began to notice in the Psalms that the authors are not embarrassed to share their emotions. Here in Psalm 3 (NRSV), David writes,

"Lord, how many are my foes" (that is, I'm feeling threatened).

"They are saying...there is no help for me in God" (they want me to believe that I can't depend on you, that you aren't a safe haven for me).

"But you are a shield around me...and the one who lifts up my head" (you are my protector and defender, and you will not let oth-ers shame me).

"I cry aloud to you..." (I can share my emotions and fears with you without embarrassment).

"You answer me..." (you are available to me when I need you).

"I am not afraid..." (I feel protected and safe).

This is all attachment language, words that a secure child would be able to express to a faithful mother or father. These are the expres-sions of someone with emotional health and confidence, which is what EFT and attachment theory are all about.

How to Pray When We Feel Afraid:

Do you ever feel vulnerable and unsafe? If so, pray Psalm 18 (NRSV), in which God is abundantly revealed to be our source of safety and security.

I love you, O LORD, my strength,
The LORD is my rock, my fortress, and my deliverer,
　my God, my rock in whom I take refuge,
　my shield, and the horn of my salvation, my stronghold.

In the first two verses alone, the psalmist fires off a dozen emotionally laden words in rapid-fire succession, proclaiming God to be the ultimate safe haven. When I first prayed this Psalm, the word "rock" jumped off the page at me, since it is the only image repeated twice. As I prayed, I suddenly visualized myself seaside in a storm, with waves threatening to carry me away. What would I do—cling to a huge rock on the beach or cling to myself? I instantly realized the absurdity of viewing myself as a rock. When skies are calm, we can cling to ourselves and pretend that we are our own source of stability. But when huge storms arise, the only logical defense is to cling to something other than ourselves, or *someone* much, much stronger. David chose to cling to God as his rock, and I am learning to do the same.

Emotionally Focused Therapy and Attachment Theory

Allow me to share a bit more of what I learned about EFT and attachment theory,[2] though I am neither a therapist nor a psychologist. Psychologists Sue Johnson and Les Greenberg coined the term "Emotionally Focused Therapy" in their 1988 book, *Emotionally Focused Therapy for Couples*.[3] Their work was based upon the groundbreaking work of psychiatrist John Bowlby (whose research and writing spanned 1944 to 1988), and the additional work of key psychologists such as Mary Ainsworth and John Gottman. Bowlby's pioneering work led to *attachment theory*, which holds that each infant must develop a secure, emotional attachment with at least one caregiver in order to grow into a confident, emotionally healthy adult. When mothers, for example, are appropriately[4] emotionally present for their infant by *attuning* to their child's emotions and needs, an *attachment bond* forms between mother and child. This bond is the secure base upon which the child can reach out in exploration of the world around her. If a distressing situation occurs, the child is sure that mother will be there as needed.

Failure to form an attachment bond results in young children who have an *insecure attachment bond* and become anxious, avoidant, or both. These patterns of attachment strongly influence (but do not determine) a person's relationships for the rest of their lives. As Bowlby put this, "Unthinking confidence in the unfailing accessibility and support of attachment figures is the bedrock on which stable and self-reliant personality is built."[5]

In layman's terms, if we are convinced to the core of our being that we are securely loved, we will be equipped to build healthy relationships with others and venture confidently into the unknowns of the future.

It is crucial to grasp that healthy attachment between a child and a caregiver is *precognitive*, before the child can even think. Thus, attachment happens on an *emotional* basis rather than mental. An infant is comforted physically and emotionally by the soothing presence of a parent long before any cognitive understanding is present. Though unable to speak or even think rationally, an infant is very able to connect through emotions and behaviors. When he is upset he lets loose loud cries and tears, demanding that his needs be met. He emotionally knows exactly what he wants, though cognitively he knows nothing at this stage in development. This is pure emotional communication.

For example, the gentle touch of a parent who responds by holding and rocking a distressed baby brings relief to the distressed child. A parent's soothing voice or singing of a lullaby can accomplish the same result. Even matching breathing rates can comfort infants. The child emotionally grasps that he is safe and not alone.

A wonderful example of this can be seen in the YouTube video uploaded by the Christian comedian Michael Jr. (www.youtube.com/watch?v=TU0f8a3Cizo). Immediately after birth, his newborn girl was placed naked on a medical exam table, and she began to shake and cry. A moment before she was in a snug womb and could hear the reassuring pulse of her mother's heartbeat, but now she was lying alone on an uncomfortable table. She is clearly upset as the nurse begins to diaper her, and her father is out of the picture.

Michael Jr. cannot hold or touch her, but he is near enough to see that his daughter is in distress and he does what he can: he simply speaks comforting words to her. Instantly she calms down and is at peace! She knows the sound of his voice, and that alone is reassuring enough that she feels safe and secure. You've really got to see the video to get the full impact.

In attachment theory, one or both parents (usually the mother) can be the source and assurance of secure love in the crucial early years of our lives. If our parents (especially in our early childhood years) were appropriately responsive when we sought their attention, protective when we were threatened, and attuned with our emotions, we formed a secure emotional base from which we could venture into the world. This is called a "safe haven" in attachment literature and EFT counseling. [6]

The focus of EFT and related therapies, however, is upon the present more than the past—upon the attachment bonds in our adult relationships because the need for secure attachment does not disappear in adulthood. So why all the discussion about the emotional climates in our families of origin? Just this: our childhood attachment experiences make adult attachments easier or more difficult. If you were raised in an emotionally healthy family, thank God for that heritage and pass it on to those in your life now and the generations to follow. If you were not raised in such a family, thank God that you now realize the importance of emotional bonding and resolve to change the generational pattern in your life and for those to follow. How we were parented is influential but not inevitable.

Theologically, we can say that God created humans to emotionally bond with others. He hard wired us with an indispensable need for faithful attachment—the Bible calls this love. Fortunately, this need can be met in a variety of ways: deep and abiding friendships, trustworthy social communities (churches), extended families, and especially in healthy marriages and nuclear families. Unfortunately, our emotional bonds can be easily damaged or even broken. It comes down to this: strong attachment bonds enable us to thrive in adulthood, whereas broken bonds threaten to disable us.

A Psychologist's Comments on this Topic:

"Rick, the concepts you are writing about are backed up by much of modern neurology and neuropsychology. Many aspects of healing, including resolving trauma, adult brain development, forgiveness, maturation, etc., are all based on an integration between the cortex (head) and the limbic system (heart), right and left hemispheres (common knowledge), and lower brain regions to upper brain regions (maturation of a person by the cortex forming strong connection to the limbic system and the brain stem).

"We see richer neural pathways of white matter (wider freeways of communication in the brain) between different areas of the brain, more effective processing of information in each region, better rational control of stronger emotions, and more emotional intelligence and 'heart' in intellectual processing. All of these things happen within the context of secure relationships (which seems to be a critical part of your writing).

Insecure relationships with people and God may lead to dis-integrated neurological experiences—when people are more split, they let God into their head (cortex), but not their hearts (limbic system and brain stem).

"I'd loved to have seen an MRI scan of Jesus' brain at work. Another attribute of his glory!"—Kenneth A. Logan, PsyD, professor of counseling, Western Seminary, Portland, Oregon

Mind you, parents need not be perfect to help their children feel securely attached. Flawlessness is not required, just consistency and predictability. Children cannot be deceived at this precognitive level and they will discern whether their parents are generally attentive, available, and reliable. If so, they likely will develop into adults with secure attachment patterns.

For instance, our middle child, Noah, was quite active and adventurous as a young child, almost to the point of fearlessness. He was, as some friends noted, "All boy." He loved to wrestle, growl, and stomp around—just like his favorite animals, dinosaurs. I used to joke that Noah thought he was a dinosaur. This created a few problems. Other children didn't always like being growled at and chased by him, but he was just being friendly, dino-style. As a result, he didn't have a lot of close friends as a young child. I occasionally worried that he would grow into a solitary adult.

As Noah grew, the opposite happened, especially in high school. And since then, Noah has tons of friends—and, thankfully, he no longer growls or chases them. He is blessed with an exceptional ability to make and keep many long-lasting relationships. He is quite confident in who he is and is secure in the reliability and longevity of his friendships. For Noah, it's once a friend, always a friend.

How did our dino-boy become a champion friend-maker and keeper? A hint of an answer came from an observation his grandmother Marcia made several times during his childhood. She said to my wife, Amy (her daughter), "Noah runs and jumps and pushes the limits, but from time to time he always looks back to make sure that you, Amy, are watching and available if needed."

Amy now recognizes in this story the essential core of attachment theory. She was the solid base, the safe haven in his life. And because he was securely attached to her, he was able to confidently explore the world and build other relationships.

Noah's behavior as a child is a great example of attachment theory in practice. Those who feel they have someone who is a protective place for them, a fortress (to use the language of the Psalms), are able to reach out with confidence and courage into an uncertain and even troubled world. They are able to build strong relationships with others because they assume that others will, in like manner, be safe and reliable.

The Power of Secure Attachment:

"Our partners powerfully affect our ability to thrive in the world. There is no way around that. Not only do they influence how we feel about ourselves but also the degree to which we believe in ourselves and whether we will attempt to achieve our hopes and dreams. Having a partner who fulfills our intrinsic attachment needs and feels comfortable acting as a secure base and safe haven can help us remain emotionally and physically healthier and live longer."—Amir Levine, MD, and Rachel S.F. Heller, MA[7]

Our Attentive, Safe, and Reliable Heavenly Father

In light of this, attend afresh to the words of the first few verses of Psalm 3:

> O Lord, how many are my foes!
>   Many are rising against me;
> many are saying to me,
>   "There is no help for you in God." *Selah*
> But you, O Lord, are a shield around me,
>   my glory, and the one who lifts up my head.
> I cry aloud to the Lord,
>   and he answers me from his holy hill. *Selah*
>   (Psalm 3:1-4 NRSV)

These few verses are just loaded with attachment images and ideas, like a heavily burdened orchard tree. The fruit is everywhere, ripe for the picking.

First, let's look at verse 1: "How many are my foes...Many are rising against me." These are words that reveal the psalmist was facing a host of troubles. His woes are not singular but plural ("foes"), and they were increasing in number ("rising").

Have you ever felt this way? Were you dodging calls from several creditors, fending off the disapproval of more than one family member, or enduring the criticisms of dozens of church members? And why is it that when things go bad, they seem to go bad in groups? Problems multiply like rabbits, and sorrow seems to hit us in sets, like waves upon the seashore. As Charles Spurgeon said, "Trouble always comes in flocks. Sorrow hath a numerous family." [8]

We all have troubles in life. Jesus promised this: "In this world you will have trouble. But take heart! I have overcome the world" (John 16:33). ("Take heart," by the way, is an emotive phrase that focuses on our feelings rather than our thoughts.) Roy Zuck writes, "Crisis, whether national or individual, reveals our human weakness and prompts us to turn to God. That's what the nation of Israel did in the wilderness. 'They cried out to the Lord in their trouble'" (Psalm 107:6). [9]

The Psalms, then, illustrate how to deal with troubles. In a world filled with both trouble and troublemakers (foes), the writer of

Psalm 3 appears confident and strong. He has a secure anchor to which he is attached, a solid rock to stand upon amidst the storm. Even as many people say to him, "There is no help for you in God," he knows this is not true. They are attempting to sever the attachment between him and God, or at least cause him to doubt that God is a secure base. The psalmist brushes off this false propaganda since Yahweh is not a god he knows in theory only but a heavenly caregiver who has always proved faithful and available in the past. He knows this God better than his adversaries do; he knows Yahweh personally and intimately.

This also happened to Jesus on the cross. His enemies mocked him, "He trusts in God. Let God rescue him now if he wants him, for he said, 'I am the Son of God'" (Matthew 27:43). This is a clear attack on and denial of the attachment bond between Jesus and his Father, because any father would rescue a true son. Even Jesus felt the sense of abandonment, saying, "My God, my God, why have you forsaken me?" (Matthew 27:46). What an intense appeal, and what vivid emotional language! In spite of the circumstance, the attachment bond between Jesus and God was so strong, so resilient, that as Jesus breathed his last breath, he returned to intimate language. His confidence in God was so personal that he returned to the most basic form of familial address and was able to say, "Father, into your hands I commit my spirit" (Luke 23:46). In the absence of a rescue in life, Jesus still trusted God as his rescuer in death. That's a secure base, a safe haven.

Job had a similar confidence in God, revealed when he said, "Though he slay me, yet will I hope in him" (Job 13:15). So did Shadrach, Meshach, and Abednego. King Nebuchadnezzar, in "furious rage" (that's an emotional phrase!), warned them:

> "Now when you hear the sound of the horn, flute, zither, lyre, harp, pipe and all kinds of music, if you are ready to fall down and worship the image I made, very good. But if you do not worship it, you will be thrown

immediately into a blazing furnace. Then what god will be able to rescue you from my hand?"

Shadrach, Meshach and Abednego replied to him, "King Nebuchadnezzar, we do not need to defend ourselves before you in this matter. If we are thrown into the blazing furnace, the God we serve is able to deliver us from it, and he will deliver us from Your Majesty's hand. But even if he does not, we want you to know, Your Majesty, that we will not serve your gods or worship the image of gold you have set up" (Daniel 3:15-18).

These three men were so confident of God's protective love that even a fiery furnace could not shake them. Now that's a secure attachment bond!

Attachment and Spiritual Formation:

"The Christian spirituality literature has a long tradition of examining attachment, encouraging people to achieve a healthy detachment (or nonattachment) from unhealthy concerns (such as fear, worry, lust, pride, selfish promotion and ceaseless striving) and connections (including possessiveness, idolatry, tyranny and more). The tradition also offers relational disciplines for cultivating healthy, ordered attachments to God and others, bringing them into better alignment so that we love what and whom we ought to love with a freedom that neither grasps nor withholds."—Susan S. Phillips[10]

The Personal Name *Yahweh*

In Psalm 3 we also can discern the evidence of a strongly connected relationship between the psalmist and God through the psalmist's use of "LORD" instead of "God."

In Hebrew, "God" is *Elohim*, the pluralized form of *El*, the common Canaanite word for deity. Among the Hebrews, it was used to refer to God in his majestic generality. "LORD," on the other hand, is the Jewish substitute for *Yahweh*, which was God's self-revelation of his own private name to Moses (Exodus 3:15). It was a personal name, used only by those who had a special relationship with God and therefore possessed the right to its use. Yahweh was an intimate name, not to be used by those to whom it was not revealed.

I noticed an example of the proper and improper use of a name in a TV drama my wife and I watched recently. During an episode of *Madame Secretary*, a politician asked Secretary of State Elizabeth McCord, "May I call you Elizabeth or do you prefer Dr. McCord?" He clearly assumed she would say, "Oh, Elizabeth is fine." Instead, she put him in his place when she responded, "Dr. McCord is fine." The message was clear: we have no personal relationship that qualifies you to use my personal name. My impersonal title will suffice.

In contrast, the psalmist opens Psalm 3 with a personal call-out to the God he knows intimately. He does this by the use of God's privately revealed name: *Yahweh*. The psalmist uses this personal name for God five times in eight verses, which highlights both the closeness he felt to God and the urgency of his situation. If my wife were calling to me from the other room and said, "Rick!" I hope I would respond at once. But if she were to say, "Rick! Rick! Rick!" I would sense she was in need and drop everything and rush to her side.

In like manner, the psalmist is certain that God will rush to his aid when needed. In fact, he is certain that Yahweh is already present, protecting and meeting his needs. He prays, "You are a shield around me, my glory, and the one who lifts up my head." Yahweh is the one, the psalmist is certain, who "answers me from his holy hill."

This is emotionally focused attachment language in a staccato burst of four images. God is not just a secure base; he also is a protective shield like those that encircled the torsos of ancient warriors. Second, God is not just one whom the psalmist honors, but God responds with mutual admiration and honor, which is what "my glory" entails. Third, God is the "lifter of the head," that is, the one who brings encouragement rather than despair, one who bestows honor rather than shame. [11] Shame may be one of the strongest of our human emotions and one of the few that God never shares. Nonetheless, God recognizes our emotional descent into shame, and he rescues and restores us as needed. Last, Yahweh "answers" the psalmist when he "cries aloud." Children who cry to their parents and receive no answer or inconsistent answers fail to establish deep attachment bonds, whereas children whose parents answer them consistently and appropriately grow strong and secure. Here we see yet another example of the deep and personal connection between the psalmist and Yahweh.

Of course, this was written down not as a mere memoir or journal but as an example for other Israelites to follow. It was included in the Psalter because feelings of trouble, opposition, abandonment, vulnerability, shame, and aloneness are universal feelings among the human race. There is neither an era nor a culture in which these feelings have not been present. So Psalm 3 can be for us, even today, a path to express these feelings openly to God and to receive from him the reassurance that he is with us, protecting us, lifting us from shame. When we lift these words to God in prayer as our own words, in the context of our own stories, expressing our own needs, the Lord hears our cries. Let's give it a try:

O Lord,...

> *Abba, Father, I call out to you by the name that Jesus used for you, a name of deep connection and intimacy: "Abba," a name that young Hebrew children use for their own loving and protective fathers. [12] In deep respect, I call out to you, my Abba.*

...how many are my foes!
   Many are rising up against me;
many are saying to me,
   "There is no help for you in God." *Selah*

> *Abba, I call out to you because my troubles seem to be grow-ing, and the people giving me problems seem to be increas-ing. They even are suggesting that you have abandoned me. That's a scary thought—but I don't believe them. I choose to believe you, because you said you will "never leave or forsake me" (Hebrews 13:5).*
>
> *So I lay before you these people who are troubling me, and I ask you to protect me from their attacks:*

_____

_____

But you, O Lord, are a shield around me,
   my glory, and the one who lifts up my head.
I cry aloud to the Lord,
   and he answers me from his holy hill. *Selah*

> *I admit to you, my Abba, that at times I feel vulnerable because*

_____

_____

> *Please, Abba, be a shield about me. I admit to you, my Father, that I now feel dishonored and ashamed because*

_____

_____

*Please be my glory and the lifter of my head. I admit to you,
dear Lord, that I need you to answer me as I ask you to
rescue me from*

_____

_____

*Please answer me from your holy hill.
Amen.*

The Huge Impact of Praying the Psalms Emotionally

"Rick, I have often thought that the relation between the Psalms and attachment theory was a neglected topic in our biblical resource literature...Your use of attachment theory is ultimately relevant for spiritual transformation, because in my experience we don't really change both heart and head (implicit & explicit) until we are secure; we tend to just change our head (explicit change).

"A pastor encouraging emotional awareness as a part of God communicating to us through our emotions and encompassing our emotions into an intimate interaction with God (making emotions part of the relationship) is huge and will create opportunities for tremendous transformation."—Kenneth A. Logan, PsyD, professor of counseling, Western Seminary, Portland, Oregon

Affirming God as Our Secure Base Through Prayer

By paying attention to emotional words and phrases, we strengthen our connections with one another—and we deepen our self-awareness. Over time, these trustworthy connections develop into protected platforms where we feel safe and valued, places to which we can return to find comfort and safety when needed.

I found that after I shared emotionally with my wife—and she, of course, received and validated those shared emotions—a sense of peace and restfulness fell upon me. I could feel my body relax, and my pulse rate became slower. I was even better able to fall asleep, secure in our bond that would help us through any storms.

David experienced exactly the same benefits after prayer:

> I lie down and sleep;
>> I wake again, for the LORD sustains me.
> I am not afraid of ten thousands of people
>> who have set themselves against me all around.
>> (Psalm 2:5-6 NRSV)

It is no surprise that Psalm 4, after the torrent of the psalmist's fearful emotions are expressed, also ends with a similar declaration of trust and the ensuing ability to sleep:

> I will both lie down and sleep in peace;
>> for you alone, O LORD, make me lie down in safety.
>> (Psalm 4:8 NRSV)

What Can We Do with Our Anger and Hatred?

It's great to be able to share deeply, on an emotional basis, with a trusted spouse or friend, and as a result be able to sleep soundly. Sleep is often a gift from God, a restorative for our souls. But what do we do when we wake up in the morning and the anger and fears return to our minds? How can we handle our wrath—and even hatred? How can we manage our desires for revenge?

By this time, you know the answer: we can take all of our feelings—both positive and negative—to God in prayer, as modeled for us by the psalmists. Here in Psalm 3, David prays,

Rise up, O LORD!
   Deliver me, O my God!
For you strike all my enemies on the cheek;
   you break the teeth of the wicked.
                    (Psalm 3:7 NRSV)

This is a repeat of the same type of request offered in the previous Psalm:

He rebukes them in his anger
   and terrifies them in his wrath…
"You will break them with a rod of iron;
   you will dash them to pieces like pottery.
                    (Psalm 2:5,9)

Who is this God who rebukes and terrifies, who feels anger and wrath? Even more, who is this God who treats people harshly, who breaks "the teeth of the wicked" and "dashes them to pieces like pottery"? What happened to the God of love, mercy, and grace?

Why is this in the Bible? Who can understand such a desire or utter such a prayer?

We have entered into dangerous territory and must exercise extreme caution; this is land upon which even angels might fear to tread. Scholars call these the "imprecatory Psalms" because they call upon God to harm or curse someone.

The curses and desires for vengeance trouble many readers, both lay and scholars alike. It is tempting to dismiss them as "old covenant" and no longer applicable in the new. But—how shocking is this?—we even find curses and imprecatory prayers in the New Testament.

Let's be honest—haven't we found anger, hatred, and the desire to curse in our own hearts? To deal with such emotions will be one of the greatest benefits of praying the Psalms, a benefit that will not only draw us closer to God but will positively transform our closest relationships. Bluntly put, if we don't learn how to identify our impulses to be angry and take revenge, we will never truly be successful in loving our family, friends, enemies (as Jesus called us to do)—and God.

Dealing with hatred and revenge, then, is a tremendous opportunity. In the next chapter, we will wade into this difficult and dangerous—yet immensely rewarding—territory.

5

Connecting with God Through Anger, Grief, and Sadness

The Psalms and Emotionally Healthy Spirituality

———— ❧ ————

"I only pray when I am in trouble. But I am in trouble all the time, and so I pray all the time."—Isaac Bashevis Singer [1]

Rise up, O LORD!
　Deliver me, O my God!
For you strike all my enemies on the cheek;
　you break the teeth of the wicked.
(Psalm 3:7 NRSV)

In the previous chapter of this book we prayed the first three-quarters of Psalm 3. It was a nice prayer, a G-rated appeal to God. It began with a rather placid plea for divine protection and a reassurance of his answer. We were nicely comforted with the reminder that God is a shield about us and that he rescues us from shame. As a result, we were able to lie down and anticipate a peaceful sleep. It was all quite lovely, calm, and pleasant, like a Sunday stroll and chat with a good friend on the way home from church, followed by an afternoon nap. If we are looking for a tranquil Psalm to read before bed, Psalm 3:1-6 hits the mark.

But suddenly, our serenity is shattered as the psalmist cries out for God to strike his "enemies on the cheek" and "break the teeth of the wicked" (Psalm 3:7).

How did calls for such inhumane, horrific violence get in the Bible? Who would have imagined that the Good Book contained such bad thoughts? Aren't we supposed to forgive our enemies rather than pray that they get hurt? And does this mean that we can use violent and vitriolic terms in our everyday speech?[2]

I can understand requests for God to judge and punish as he sees fit (otherwise, justice has no ultimate content), but to ask him to break people's jaws or shatter their teeth seems extremely cruel. Have you ever desired such pain upon anyone—even your worst enemy? (I know from personal experience the pain of broken teeth since my two front teeth have been broken several times, mostly from sports injuries.) Have you longed for the children of your foes to suffer, as the psalmist prays in Psalm 109:9-10? The God in this Psalm sounds more like a sadistic mafia don than a forgiving friend.

Years ago I began to read a legal thriller in which the gang leader in a prison took a new convict and broke off all his teeth on a steel bathroom sink. That image was so violent, so disgusting to me that I not only stopped reading the book—I threw it in the trash. I didn't want anyone else to be exposed to such appalling cruelty. Yet here in the Bible is a prayer asking God to do the same—to be the divine brutalizer.

To be blunt, prayers that ask God to "break the teeth" or to make someone's children "wandering beggars" disturb me. But in saying so, do I imply that I am morally superior compared to these psalmists? Such a thought also sickens me. What a conundrum!

Curses Are Not Rare in the Psalms

What can we do with such violent and vengeful thoughts? Shall we excise them from our hymnals and liturgies, as the editors of the Revised Common Lectionary (Episcopal Church) and the Liturgy of the Hours (Roman Catholic Church) have done? Shall we treat them as metaphors (this seems to be C.S. Lewis's solution[3])? Or shall we skip the difficult passages when we pray the Psalms?

Dan Allender and Tremper Longman III confront this difficulty head-on in their insightful book *The Cry of the Soul*:

> Some believers cringe from this language of desperation and rage, even though they have the model of the psalmist. "The psalmist didn't have Christ, but we do—so we can't be lonely, angry, or afraid!"
>
> But this is presumption, not faith. The laments of the Psalms encourage us to risk the danger of speaking boldly and personally to the Lord of the universe.[4]

So if we should not avoid praying the difficult Psalms, what other options do we have? Can we assume that this verse in Psalm 3 is an exception to the rule, an oddity in an otherwise loving and merciful book of spiritual poems? Further study reveals this maneuver does us no good because many, many Psalms contain at least one vengeful or violent thought, while others seem to specialize in those themes.

The Real Problem with the Desire for Revenge:

Old Testament scholar Walter Brueggemann notes, "The real theological problem, I submit, is not that vengeance is there in the Psalms, but that it is here in our midst. And that it is there and here only reflects how attuned the Psalter is to what goes on among us…The articulation of vengeance leads us to new awareness about ourselves."[5]

Consider, for instance, just the first dozen Psalms. How many of these contain curses or requests that ask God to judge the evildoing of the psalmists' enemies and punish them accordingly? Take a moment, a *Selah*, open your Bible and slowly read the first twelve Psalms. Place a mark beside any verse that contains a prayer that implies God will judge, harm, or punish the psalmists' opponents. (Spoiler alert: I found that eleven out of the first twelve Psalms qualified to be so marked.)

Or if you prefer, read aloud (I dare you) just these few examples from the first dozen Psalms and try to feel the depth of the psalmists' emotions:

> You will break them with a rod of iron;
>   you will dash them to pieces like pottery.
>   (Psalm 2:9)

> Strike all my enemies on the jaw;
>   break the teeth of the wicked.
>   (Psalm 3:7)

> The arrogant cannot stand
>   in your presence.
> You hate all who do wrong;
>   you destroy those who tell lies.
>   (Psalm 5:5-6)

> All my enemies will be overwhelmed with shame and anguish;
>   they will turn back and suddenly be put to shame.
>   (Psalm 6:10)

So how can we understand the use of numerous angry curses in the Psalms? Here is my conclusion: curses are not rare in the Psalms because undeserved suffering is not rare in real life. All of us have been hurt—most of us tremendously so—and instantly feel the desire to strike back verbally, if not physically (which is just what a curse entails). Thus, angry curses are frequent in the Psalms because the instinct toward revenge is a frequent emotion in the hearts of humans.

When we are harmed without cause, we feel justified in desiring revenge. It seems to be hard-wired into human rationality that "eye for eye, tooth for tooth [yes, here's that broken-tooth image again]" (Exodus 21:24) is morally right. Even young kids will strike back when struck by another, thinking, *It's only fair.* In legal terms, this moral position is called *lex talionis,* or the "law of retaliation." It is one of the bases of secular law, including laws in the United States. If we cause someone to lose an eye, fortunately our more civilized society won't actually demand an eye from us, but it still will demand appropriate compensation. If we damage someone's property, we are responsible to pay for the repairs.

When we are hurt, we instinctively desire that the offending party hurt also, so it follows that when we are tremendously hurt, we want the offender to tremendously hurt. And I repeat: most of us have been tremendously hurt in this life.

I still remember the day this dawned upon me. Before one of our weekend services, a couple stopped me in the lobby with downcast faces. They said, "Rick, do you know what today is?"

"No," I responded.

"Today is the one-year anniversary of our granddaughter's drowning in a pool. You did the memorial, remember?"

"Yes, I remember the memorial, but I had forgotten the exact date. I'm again so sorry for your loss." We then shared together a few special moments of tears, memories, and prayers, and then I watched in awe as they walked away, hand in hand. Couples who survive such an event—and remain happily married—are truly extraordinary people.

I was still thinking about and praying for them as I stepped onto the stage to deliver my sermon. I was deeply sad for their *sorrow anniversary,* as I came to call it. Every year, for the rest of their lives, this date will bring pain and grief. As I looked out upon more than a thousand faces, it hit me that every single family has probably experienced similarly tremendous pain in life—and some even more than once. As I began my sermon, I was thinking completely different thoughts in the background of my mind: *What amazing, resilient people you all are—that you can be hurt so deeply yet carry on. What sadness and sorrow you must carry beneath the veneer of your Sunday smiles. What a testimony to your faith that you still choose to follow God after such dark valleys.* On that Sunday, my respect for "average Christians" grew a thousand-fold.

That morning it hit me that every adult in our church probably has several sorrow anniversaries. Everyone experiences—either personally or within their close circle of family and friends—major distress-inducing events. Such awful events might include:

- the death of a family member or friend
- the agony of watching a loved one battle cancer or some other disease
- the rending of a marriage through some type of unfaithfulness or divorce
- feelings of abandonment
- children in rebellion
- a suicide
- a loved one with mental illness
- the loss of a job or a financial collapse
- pain from physical or emotional abuse

Here's one example from my own life. I never anticipated that pastoring a large church would bring my heart such grief—simply due to the laws of mathematics. When our church grew quickly, so did the number of grief-producing occasions. Thus, for the last twenty years I have shepherded many church families through the sorrow that accompanies childhood deaths, suicides, traffic accidents, casualties of war, cancers, and on and on. Don't misunderstand me—I'm not complaining. I considered it an honor to accompany those families as God walked them through the valley of the shadow of death (Psalm 23:4). Nonetheless, when they hurt, I hurt. So I've hurt a lot.

I guess I could have been an emotionally distant pastor, keeping a safe distance from the sorrows of others. But that isn't how God wired me. Our church was built on two of my key values: loving people one at a time and treating members as I would want my own children to be treated. In other words, I cared about our parishioners, which also entailed that I rejoiced when they rejoiced and mourned when they mourned (Romans 12:15).

Over time, this took a toll on my spirit. Sorrow seemed to not merely add but multiply (grief counselors call this "compound" or "accumulated" losses[6]). I would look over our congregation and feel deeply for them, as a shepherd feels for his sheep. But each memorial service gouged out an additional chunk from my heart, to the point that I began to feel permanent heartache.

Praying the Psalms helped me enormously because I could see that I was not alone in my suffering as a leader. As the Psalms reveal, King David was often overcome by sorrow and fear, as were Solomon, Asaph, the sons of Korah, and other psalmists who remain unnamed. Everyone suffers in this life; no one is exempt. As Christian psychologists Tim Clinton and Gary Sibcy put this, "Sooner or later, life trashes our trophies."[7]

African-American Spirituals and the Psalms:

"Suffering is a prominent theme in both the Psalms and the African American spirituals. In the Psalms, suffering is usually expressed through the genre of lament, or a petition for deliverance from some kind of distress based on God's faithfulness and the power to save in history. Scholars disagree whether these psalms depict a movement from suffering to hope and joy, or if they hold suffering and hope in tension, affirming the need for and possibility of joy in the midst of suffering. The spirituals also seem simultaneously to affirm both suffering and joyous hope."—Elizabeth Backfish[8]

As I prayed the Psalms, I felt the psalmists' deep pain pulsate from the pages, and I realized that sorrow drove their requests for violent justice.

> Strike them with terror, LORD;
>   let the nations know they are only mortal.
>   (Psalm 9:20)

> Break the arm of the wicked man (Psalm 10:15).

> The LORD examines the righteous,
>   but the wicked, those who love violence,
>   he hates with a passion.
> On the wicked he will rain
>   fiery coals and burning sulfur;
>   a scorching wind will be their lot.
>   (Psalm 11:5-6)

This is not nice language or friendly rhetoric. These are not prayers hoping for repentance and reconciliation; they are curses calling down God's hurtful, brutal wrath. These are not the prayers one learns in Sunday school.

And we haven't even got to the worst one yet.

The Rivers of Babylon

> By the rivers of Babylon, there we sat down,
>   Ye-eah we wept, when we remembered Zion. [9]

So sang the pop group Boney M in the hauntingly beautiful "Rivers of Babylon," one of my favorite classic rock songs. Yet they didn't write it, didn't all really sing it, and it is doubtful whether the producer or the public ever understood it. [10]

After "Rivers of Babylon" was released in 1978, it became the top hit in the United Kingdom for five weeks and peaked at 30 on the

United States pop charts. It's a peculiar song, completely composed of lyrics taken from Psalm 137:1-4 and Psalm 19:14, yet it became a big hit in England for this secular band. Old Testament scholar John Goldingay has argued that "Rivers of Babylon" was a Rastafarian song calling for social justice against the modern-day "Babylons," Britain and America. As Goldingay summed up, "Ironically, we British who listened to and sang the song never realized that it was about us, that we were Babylon. Perhaps the BBC would have banned it if we had realized." [11]

This would have been the case even more had the public known the last lines of Psalm 137, two of the most shocking sentences found anywhere in the Bible. Eugene Peterson calls Psalm 137 "The Scandal of the Psalter" [12]:

> Daughter Babylon, doomed to destruction,
>   happy is the one who repays you
>   according to what you have done to us.
> Happy is the one who seizes your infants
>   and dashes them against the rocks.
>   (Psalm 137:8-9)

Here the Bible seems to cross the line into child abuse and immoral bloodlust, to anger run amuck. How can the psalmist even suggest that viciously murdering innocent children would be a happy event?

Psalms of Curses, AKA the Imprecatory Psalms

Though a majority of the Psalms contain some curse or request that God judge evildoers, there are several in which cursing is the central theme—and Psalm 137 takes the cake. Scholars call these the *Imprecatory Psalms*, which is a fancy way of saying Cursing Psalms. When we pray these Psalms, God forces us to deal with emotions we often avoid in public: anger, hatred, and the desire for revenge.

But this is hard to do. Many of the imprecatory Psalms are, to use C.S. Lewis's term, "shockingly alien" to both our modern and

Christian sensibilities. Lewis said, "We find in the Psalms expressions of a cruelty more vindictive and a self-righteousness more complete than anything in the classics."[13] So should we pray the cursing Psalms? Yes, suggests John Goldingay, because the New Testament doesn't censor them (see John 2:17 and Acts 1:20). In addition, Jesus doesn't shy away from calling down curses ("Woe to you, teachers of the law and Pharisees, you hypocrites!" Matthew 23:13ff.), and the martyrs in Revelation 6:10 pray for God to execute judgment.[14]

The Psalms are good for us because such feelings are present in all of our lives at different times and in different measures. Many of us, though, have not been taught to deal with anger and hatred in emotionally healthy ways. Even worse, some of us haven't been taught to identify them at all. For instance, many Christians have assumed that anger is always a sin, so any angry feelings are denied or ignored. Allender and Longman claim, "The Psalms provoke us to move out of denial. Christians are particularly adept at numbing themselves against painful emotions."[15] I agree with their assessment, and note that secular people are also very adept at this, choosing numbing options such as alcohol, eating, drugs, entertainment, and gambling. All of us—saints or seculars—seem to be experts at repressing and stuffing our emotions away, deep down in our hearts, with the hope that they will suffocate and die there. Instead, buried emotions fester, grow, and become cancerous infections in our souls.

Much of this we carry around like weighty cysts within our hearts, completely unknown to those around us. As a result, many Christians have learned how to bottle-up negative emotions and live public lives of false equanimity. We are like the Reverend Dimmesdale in Nathaniel Hawthorne's masterpiece, *The Scarlett Letter*. On the outside he appeared to be the epitome of Christian virtue, but on the inside he was slowly dying from deeply hidden emotional turmoil over his unconfessed sin.

Like Dimmesdale, many of us look good on the outside but are suffering on the inside. This is especially true of pastors—or at least it was of me. During almost forty years of ministry, I often swallowed my anger toward and disappointment in people, thinking that unleashing my true feelings would drive them from the church. I kept all manner of negative emotions deep inside, telling myself that it was Christlike and forgiving to "overlook an offense" (Proverbs 19:11).

In a manner of speaking, I sacrificed my emotional integrity for what I perceived would be best for the church: keeping the peace. The really ironic part is that, in the end, those people left the church anyway. I had sacrificed my emotional integrity for nothing.

In hindsight, I erred greatly by hiding my unpleasant feelings from others and myself. However, I'm not the only pastor who has fallen on this sword. Many of my generation behaved in the same way, having been counseled to keep the peace and to avoid confrontation ("turn the other cheek") if at all possible. We were emotionally blind guides following other emotionally blind guides.

Finally, the blinders came off when I reread a life-changing book by Peter Scazzero, *The Emotionally Healthy Church*. (With embarrassment I confess to having read the book several years before my wakeup call, before which I was unable to grasp its importance.) This book, along with the excellent sequels, became the *third stream of emotional insight* that, at the right time, filled my life with desperately needed truth about healthy emotions and spirituality.

Iceberg Christians

In *The Emotionally Healthy Church*, Scazzero tells the story of eight years of driven, emotionally unaware ministry that almost destroyed his church. Peter and his wife, Geri, after one year of marriage, moved to the New York City borough of Queens to start a new church. He writes:

> We always seemed to have too much to do in too little time. While the church was an exciting place to be, it was not a joy to be in leadership—especially for my wife, Geri, and me...We knew something was missing. Our hearts were shrinking. Church leadership felt like

a heavy burden. We were gaining the whole world by doing a great work for God while at the same time losing our souls. [16]

Their church, New Life Fellowship, began in 1987, just six years before my wife and I moved to Rocklin, California, to begin our new church. Like Scazzero's fellowship, our church grew rapidly—in ten years Adventure Christian Church grew from zero to over five thousand in attendance. And like Scazzero, I lost myself in the process. I often said to other church leaders, "The one verse that best expresses the life of a megachurch pastor is, 'I die daily'" (1 Corinthians 15:31 KJV). Scazzero fell into the same trap and expressed the problem this way:

> Jesus does call us to die to ourselves. "If anyone would come after me, he must deny himself and take up his cross and follow me" (Mark 8:34). The problem was that we had died to the wrong things. We mistakenly thought that dying to ourselves for the sake of the Gospel meant dying to self-care, to feelings of sadness, to anger, to grief, to doubt, to struggles, to our healthy dreams and desires, and to passions we had enjoyed before our marriage. [17]

Rather than dying to self in a Christlike manner, Scazzero was killing and burying his emotions. But instead of getting rid of them, these negative emotions remained within him like heavy ballast weighing down his life.

Scazzero describes this with a vivid word picture: "My life was like an iceberg, with many weightier portions hidden under the surface of the waterline. Even though they were beneath the surface, they dominated my visible life." [18] In his sequel, *Emotionally Healthy Spirituality*, Scazzero calls this "tip-of-the-iceberg spirituality," the tendency to not admit the deep layers of emotions beneath our conscious awareness. [19]

Change That Hurts—and Heals

The neglect of those deep emotional layers created other problems. Scazzero's church, again like ours, went through a terrible split. Rather than publicly confronting those responsible, Scazzero tried to put a positive spin on things. Listen to what he said to the church after the split, and his later reflections about his comments:

> "Isn't it amazing how God uses our sins to expand his kingdom? Now we have two churches instead of one," I proclaimed. "Now more people can come into a personal relationship with Jesus. If any of you want to go over to that new church, may God's blessings be upon you."
>
> I lied.
>
> I was going to be like Jesus (at least the image of Jesus I imagined him to be), even if it killed me. It did—in my inward self.
>
> My hell was that inside I was deeply wounded and angry. These feelings gave way to hate. My heart did not hold any forgiveness. I was full of rage, and I couldn't get rid of it.
>
> When I was alone in my car, just the thought of what had happened would trigger a burst of anger, a knot in my stomach. Within seconds, curse words would follow, flying almost involuntarily from my mouth. [20]

I can totally relate with the majority of this passage. [21] I sorrowed deeply over the friendships I lost when people left our church, yet I masked those feelings in upbeat phrases like, "We're helping many churches grow in our region." In fact, it took me several years before I was even able to call the exodus from our church a "church split" and confess my part in it (sadly, many of those that engineered it or participated in it have yet to do so).

I too was filled with anger and rage, but knew no acceptable way to deal with or heal it. I felt like Atlas, with a huge weight upon my shoulders and no place to lay it down. A few times, as I lay in bed feeling the heaviness upon my heart, I thought, *Is this what middle-aged men feel just before they have a heart attack?*

But I kept those feelings to myself and away from our church, my wife, and even God. I had responsibilities; people were counting on me. I had to be strong and keep a steady course through the storms—after all, my name is Stedman (a derivative of Stead-man).

For Scazzero, the wakeup call came from his wife. After nine years of marriage and eight years in their new church, she said:

> "Pete, I love you but I'm leaving the church…I no longer respect your leadership."
>
> I was visibly shaken and didn't know what to say or do. I felt shamed, alone, and angry.
>
> I tried raising my voice to intimidate her: "That is out of the question…"
>
> There was long pause of silence. Then she uttered the words that changed the power balance in our marriage permanently: "Pete, I quit…I love you, Pete. But the truth is, I would be happier separated than married."
>
> She was calm and resolute in her decision. I was enraged…I wanted to die. This was going to require me to change![22]

Though my wife never decided to leave our church, in hindsight she had every right to. After the first ten years of rapid growth, our church entered a decade of difficulty. At the time, I believed a large portion of the problem was spiritual warfare, but I now see that another big problem was the lack of emotional maturity in church leadership—including me. Bluntly put, it was impossible to maintain spiritual vitality without also growing in emotional excellence.

As Scazzero summarized, "Embracing the truth about the emotional parts of myself unleashed nothing short of a revolution in my understanding of God, Scripture, the nature of Christian maturity, and the role of the church. I can no longer deny the truth that emotional and spiritual maturity are inseparable. [23]

What Does Spiritual and Emotional Maturity Look Like?

Scazzero answers this question about what maturity looks like with "The Six Principles of an Emotionally Healthy Church":

- *Principle 1:* Look beneath the surface.

- *Principle 2:* Break the power of the past.

- *Principle 3:* Live in brokenness and vulnerability.

- *Principle 4:* Receive the gift of limits.

- *Principle 5:* Embrace grieving and loss.

- *Principle 6:* Make incarnation your model for loving well.

I highly recommend that every pastor read, reread, and discuss *The Emotionally Healthy Church* in a small group of other trusted pastors. I also think it would be a great goal to have all church leaders—and, if married, their spouses—read and discuss its principles.

Or, we can pray the same topics as they inevitably arise in the Psalms.

In Psalms 5 and 6, the next prayers on our journey through the Psalms, the psalmist begins with a stirring plea:

> Give ear to my words, O Lord,
>   give heed to my sighing.
> Listen to the sound of my cry,
>   my King and my God,
>   for to you I pray.
>
> (Psalm 5:1-2 NRSV)

In like manner, Psalm 6 starts on a very emotional level:

> O LORD, do not rebuke me in your anger,
>   or discipline me in your wrath.
> Be gracious to me, O LORD, for I am languishing;
>   O LORD, heal me, for my bones are shaking with terror.
>   (Psalm 6:1-2 NRSV)

This is a good example of Scazzero's *Principle 1*: looking beneath the surface of one's circumstances and attending to the emotions deep within. Emotionally mature spirituality begins when we learn to admit and identify our emotions. The psalmists are experts at this. Here are just a few of the strongly emotional words from these four verses:

- sighing
- listen
- cry
- rebuke
- anger
- wrath
- languishing
- shaking
- terror

Once again I am struck by the emotional virtuosity of the psalmists. They have extensive affective vocabularies—far more so than we are likely to find in even seasoned Christians today. Think about it: when was the last time you used the word *languishing* or people confided to you that their "bones are shaking with terror"?

To go beneath the surface is to pay attention to what is going on in our hearts, which lends itself perfectly to prayer. First, let's read an emotional phrase from the Psalms, and then pray it:

O LORD, give heed to my sighing…

> *Lord, on the outside I act like I have it all together, but on the inside I am sighing. I am tired, weary, worn out. I'm tired because:*

_____

_____

Listen to the sound of my cry…

> *Lord, I need to unburden my heart, to reveal my struggles to someone. Will you be my confidant? My counselor? My friend? My listener? I'm crying because:*

_____

_____

LORD, I am languishing…

> *Lord, I am in pain—pain that doesn't seem to end. I feel weak and helpless. I am languishing because I can't get out of this situation:*

_____

_____

O LORD, heal me, for my bones are shaking with terror…

> *Lord, I'm coming apart on the inside. I'm terrified and afraid that something like this may happen:*

_____

_____

Help me, Lord. Do not reject me because of these emotions
I am feeling. I give them to you and ask for your healing,
in your time. Amen.

Principle 2 is breaking the power of the past. In other words, we are to identify and stop the patterns of generational sin. In its positive sense, this is to identify the healthy patterns of one's family or culture and to use those patterns for strength or guidance in the present.

A positive use of the past, for example, can be seen in the Psalms that recount the past actions of the Lord, such as Psalms 22 and 135:

> In you our ancestors trusted;
>   they trusted, and you delivered them.
> To you they cried, and were saved;
>   in you they trusted, and were not put to shame.
>   (Psalm 22:4-5 NRSV)

> For I know that the LORD is great...
> He it was who struck down the firstborn of Egypt...
> he sent signs and wonders
>   into your midst, O Egypt,
>   against Pharaoh and all his servants...
> and gave their land as a heritage,
>   a heritage to his people Israel.
>   (Psalm 135:5,8-9,12)

This is the benefit of having parents and ancestors who were sincere believers: they experienced God's goodness in times of need and God's answers to prayer. As we learn these familial accounts of God's help and provision, we are encouraged that God will come through for us also. When the psalmists reflect, in prayer, about God's actions on behalf of Israel, they are gathering strength from the positive generational patterns.

In the New Testament, Mary's "Magnificat" is a fantastic example of this. There she looks back to the positive examples in her ancestors' past to strengthen her resolve for the future. And, by the way, her prayer is filled with quotations and references from the Psalms. Mary literally reacts to the annunciation of Jesus' birth by praying the Psalms!

> "My soul magnifies the Lord...
> The Mighty One has done great things for me...
> He has helped his servant Israel,
>   in remembrance of his mercy,
> according to the promise he made to our ancestors,
>   to Abraham and his descendants forever."
>   (Luke 1:46,49,54-55 NRSV)

Like Mary, when good things happen in our lives, we can pause for a moment and thank God for his goodness in the present as well as the past. *Selah.*

On the other hand, life is not always good, and the past can continue to haunt us. Because of this, some Psalms help us face the negatives from our past in order to break their power over the present. A great example of this is David's famous admission:

> Indeed, I was born guilty,
>   a sinner when my mother conceived me.
>   (Psalm 51:5 NRSV)

Whether negative or positive, the past is a huge weight that influences our present, so it must be identified and either corrected or co-opted.

Take a moment and pray about your family's spiritual past.

> *Lord, I am blessed to be part of a long line of believers.*
> *Strengthen me by reminding me of the ways you have*
> *been faithful in my family's past:*

_____

_____

Or you might pray,

> *Lord, I do not come from a family of strong believers. In fact,*
> *my family has some generational patterns that are quite*
> *unhealthy and even sinful, such as*

_____

_____

> *Please help me, God, to stop these patterns of generational*
> *sin and to begin a new legacy for those who will follow. I*
> *ask you to make me into a person who*

_____

_____

> *Amen.*

Principles 3 through 6

Now that we understand the basic method of praying the Psalms, it will suffice to provide just a few Psalms, and prayers based on those Psalms, to illustrate the final four of Scazzero's six principles of mature spirituality.

Principle 3 is to live in brokenness and vulnerability. This is clearly evident in Psalm 6:

> I am worn out from my groaning.
> All night long I flood my bed with weeping
>   and drench my couch with tears.

My eyes grow weak with sorrow;
they fail because of all my foes.

(Psalm 6:6-7)

I don't think I have ever heard a strong Christian leader speak with as much vulnerable, emotional honesty as does this psalmist—especially about weeping. I know that I am embarrassed when I cry and try to stop the tears if I can.

But during one really difficult season in our church, I found myself weeping uncontrollably in front of my family—as we watched the movie *Evan Almighty*. This comedy probably has never brought anyone else to tears, except maybe tears of laughter. As Evan (the Noah-esque character, played by Steve Carell) tried to obey God's instructions and build the ark, everyone thought he was crazy. In spite of this, he kept the course, even if he had to do it alone.

As I watched the movie, it hit me like a ton of bricks that I was attempting to do the same. God had clearly told me to persevere in my role as senior pastor, though some friends were judging and abandoning me. My crying, like the psalmists, was "because of grief" and "filled my handkerchief with tears."

Are you now going through a tearful, grief-filled season? If so, pray the following prayer, based on Psalm 6:7. If not, is someone you love sorrowful? In that case, change the voice of this prayer from first to third person and pray it for him or her.

> *Lord, I'm not too proud to admit that I cry at times. In fact, sometimes I can't stop crying. I've lost some dear things in my life, and the grief is as intense as if a loved one has died. Lord, I'm weeping because I'm so sad over the loss of:*

_____

_____

Amen.

Principle 4 is to receive the gift of limits. This means that we will have reasonable and healthy boundaries in our lives. Rather than feeling that we never have the right to say no to any request, we will be able to say no when needed and yes only when we truly want to do so. We will not be workaholics who sacrifice our physical and familial health on the altar of success.

In addition, we will discover the limits of our competencies. For instance, we learn that it is our job to pray and God's job to answer the prayer as he sees fit. As we pray the Psalms and ask God to judge and take vengeance on those who have harmed us, we learn an astonishing truth: it's not a sin to want those who hurt us to hurt in return. Allender and Longman go even further: "It is appropriate to pray for a specific person to be broken, humbled, and brought low in order to see their evil destroyed...it is what the psalmist prayed for in wishing harm on his enemy." [24] In the New Testament the apostle Paul mentions that a man called Alexander the metalworker "did me a great deal of harm." But rather than harming him in return, Paul entrusts vengeance to God: "The Lord will repay him for what he has done" (2 Timothy 4:14). In a similar fashion, the psalmist prays:

> You destroy those who speak lies;
>   the Lord abhors the bloodthirsty and deceitful.
> But I, through the abundance of your steadfast love,
>   will enter your house,
> I will bow down toward your holy temple
>   in awe of you.
> Lead me, O Lord, in your righteousness
>   because of my enemies;
>   make your way straight before me.
>   (Psalm 5:6-8)

I love this Psalm because the writer realizes his limitations. It was his job to tell God about those who were lying, and then to give that to God in prayer and worship ("I will enter your house...and bow down…in awe of you"). It was not his responsibility to dispense judgment or punishment, but instead to pray.

Let's try this:

> *Lord, I'm so mad because some people have been lying to me. They have been saying:*

_____

_____

> *Lord, I'd really like you to prevent them from further deception, and especially self-deception. Fill them with your truth.*
> *Therefore, I relinquish any plans for revenge on my own. I put them and these pains in your hands and ask that your will be done. Amen.*

Of course, the Psalms are full of *Principle 5*, which is to embrace grieving and loss. This can be seen lexically: *grief* and *grieve* appear 9 times, not to mention other words such as *anguish, cry, mourning,* and *weeping.* By my count there are over 159 occurrences of grief-related emotional expressions in the Psalms. (For a general list of these words in the Psalms, see appendix 2, part 3.)

An example of dealing with grief is Psalm 6:7:

> My eyes waste away because of grief;
> they grow weak because of all my foes.

Emotionally healthy spirituality entails that we admit and face our sorrows instead of denying or ignoring them. A much healthier response is to take these heartaches and losses to God in prayer.

> *Lord, I've lost some dear things in my life, and the grief is as intense as if a loved one has died. Lord, I feel like I'm wasting away because I'm so sad over the loss of:*

_____

_____

(Dealing with sorrow, loss, and grief recovery are massive subjects, well beyond the scope of this book. I have included a few resources in a footnote for further reference.) [25]

Finally, *Principle 6* is to make incarnation our model for loving well. Since this is a principle based on the New Testament doctrine of the Incarnation, the coming of Jesus as the Messiah in the flesh, we might assume at first that this principle has little presence in the Psalms.

However, the opposite is the case. The Psalms often use the words *messiah*, *savior*, and *king*, which can all be interpreted as foreshadows of Christ. In addition, many verses from the Psalms are quoted in the New Testament as prophecies fulfilled in the life of Jesus, often from the lips of Jesus himself. Finally, Jesus quoted from the Psalms on at least eleven occasions, possibly alluded to them many more times, and even prayed them in his greatest time of crisis. In other words, the incarnation of Jesus is both foretold and modeled for us in the Psalms.

A perfect depiction of this can be found in Mark's Gospel, when Jesus said,

> "Haven't you read this passage of Scripture:
> 'The stone the builders rejected
>   has become the cornerstone;
> the Lord has done this,
>   and it is marvelous in our eyes'?"
> (Mark 12:10-11)

This quotation is from Psalm 118:22-23, and is used by Jesus after his parable of the tenants (Matthew 21:42; Mark 12:10-11; Luke 20:17). Plus, it is quoted in both Acts 4:11 and 1 Peter 2:7 and is alluded to in Ephesians 2:20.

Most profoundly, Jesus was literally praying the Psalms when on the cross: "My God, My God, why have you forsaken me?" (Psalm 22:1, quoted in Matthew 27:46 and Mark 15:34), and "Into your hands I commit my spirit" (Psalm 31:5, quoted in Luke 23:46). In the words of Holocaust martyr Dietrich Bonhoeffer, "Jesus died on the cross with the words of the Psalter on his lips." [26]

Think about it: what would you pray during your last moments on earth? The fact that Jesus chose to quote the Psalms in his prayers at a time of such significant pain and sorrow is strong evidence that he was very familiar with the Psalms. In his greatest moment of need, the Psalms perfectly expressed his deepest emotions to God. In like manner, we can follow this incarnational model. The Psalms can be of great help to us in our most intense moments of want, especially if we have saturated ourselves with Scripture beforehand by praying the Psalms.

In sum, the Psalms foreshadow Jesus, foretell specific facts about his life, and exemplify for us how to pray during life's most difficult moments. They are full of incarnational models for living well.

Dealing with Fear

Before we conclude this chapter, I feel the need to stress that praying the Psalms is no cure-all, no spiritual bromide that permanently removes the pain of fear, grief, and hate. Instead, as we pray the Psalms day by day and learn to share our emotions with God, we learn that he listens and answers prayer in both little and big ways. Over time, these accumulated assurances of God's availability and helpfulness do, in fact, lighten our loads.

As an example, allow me to share a personal story about my own struggle with fear and how God answers prayer. As a child I had "night terrors," bad dreams during which I would loudly cry out for help. But try as they might, my parents couldn't wake me up. After some trial and error, they finally found that leading me to the bathroom (still asleep) and splashing cold water on my face would do the trick.

These dreams diminished in frequency as my childhood progressed, but still happened occasionally during my elementary school years. Then, I went to my first junior-high church camp where I discovered the reality of a God who answers desperate prayers.

About a dozen of us seventh grade boys were assigned to a cabin, which was really more like an open carport. I immediately saw that creepy and dangerous things could get into our sleeping area.

The first night—I kid you not—our counselor decided to tell ghost stories. After about an hour, he finished his storytelling and ordered lights out. We all were scared and afraid to go to sleep.

Fortunately, my sleeping bag was next to his, so I reasoned that any bad things from the dark woods would get the campers lying on the fringes first. I was reasonably safe. That is, until one boy on the outer rim admitted his fear (an act of courage in itself) and said to our counselor, "I'm scared! Can I move my sleeping bag closer to yours?"

The counselor responded, "Sure. You other boys scoot out a little so he can move his bag next to mine."

Now I was closer to the edge but still fairly secure. But then another boy admitted the same fear and moved his bag, and another, and another. Eventually, I found myself on the outside of the circle of sleeping bags, and I was petrified. I knew I might have a night terror even if I were still next to our counselor, but lying on the outside guaranteed it. I was scared to death.

But I had heard that day about a prayer-answering God who was near to us, our helper in times of trouble (Psalm 9:9). I thought, "God, I need you right now! Please protect me from wild animals and scary things from the dark. And even more, don't let me have a night terror tonight. In fact, please help me and take them away forever."

And he did just that! I never again had a night terror.

God indeed answers prayers, and the memory of this event gives me confidence that God still listens to and answers prayer. As you pray the Psalms and share your deepest feelings with God, over time you will also grow in confidence. You will build your own history of prayers to and answers from God, which will strengthen you through many dark nights still to come.

The Heart of the Matter

In a world filled with denial and repression, it is a huge accomplishment to learn how to deal honestly and constructively with anger, hatred, and fear. When we learn to identify these emotions and express them to God in prayer, we take big steps toward emotionally healthy spirituality.

As we practice taking these raw and sensitive emotions to God by praying the Psalms, we have almost reached the heart of the matter that will help us draw closer to God and to others. Plus, it will even help us grow to accept and love ourselves more.

So what is the heart of the matter? It is what I like to call *the secret that emotionally saved my marriage*, and it has the potential to rescue and deepen all of our important relationships. If you would like to grow closer to those you love—parents, spouse, children, friends—this secret may be the solution you have been searching for. It is to the heart of the matter that we turn in the next chapter.

6

Does God Feel Loved by Me?

The Psalms and Attunement

———— ✤ ————

"God behaves in the Psalms in ways he is not allowed to
behave in systematic theology."—Sebastian Moore[1]

Rise up, O LORD, in your anger;
    lift yourself up against the fury of my enemies…
God is my shield,
    who saves the upright in heart.
God is a righteous judge,
    and a God who has indignation every day.
                     (Psalm 7:6,10-11 NRSV)

What are human beings that you are mindful of them,
    mortals that you care for them?
Yet you have made them a little lower than God,
    and crowned them with glory and honor.
                     (Psalm 8:4-5 NRSV)

During our emotional journey through the Psalms, our emphasis has been to train our eyes to pick out emotional words and
phrases. We have turned to God in prayer, asking him to reveal
whether these emotions can be found in our own hearts or in the

hearts of those we love. We have grown in our ability to pray the Psalms for ourselves and for others emotionally.

But expressing our emotions is not enough.

Identifying and sharing our emotions with God in prayer is a great start, but it is not enough to reach the higher levels of love and connection with God. The same is true with our relationships with others. There is one key step that can still be achieved, the stage that brings us to new heights of closeness with God and with those we love. It is the heart of the matter regarding relational closeness, and it is the secret that saved my marriage emotionally. It is also the secret that has deepened my relationship with God.

The Single Most Important Truth I Have Ever Learned About Marriage

One might assume that after twenty-seven years of marriage I would have my wife figured out. I would know her likes and dislikes, and I would do my best to make her happy. Sadly, the truth is that I still have a long way to go as a husband, which frustrates both her and me.

Giving Amy my full attention is one area in which I continually mess up. My excuse has been that, like many people today, I can multitask. I like accomplishing things, so if I can accomplish two at once, that's even better. But while I may be happy about this, my wife often is not. Especially when it comes to listening.

I can watch TV, for instance, and also listen to Amy. I can glance at the mail or read a book and still hear and even repeat what she says. Of course, she doesn't like anything less than my full attention, so over the years she often has said to me, "Rick, you aren't listening to me." To which I would reply, "Yes I am. You said…" (Here I would quote word for word what she had just said.)

Did this make her happy or more frustrated? Much to my confusion, this left her even more bothered than before. If she wasn't upset previously, she was by now.

I never understood this. She claimed I wasn't listening, though I clearly was able to prove that I was. Yet I seemed to lose points in these exchanges rather than gain them. Never once did she respond, "What a brilliant man I married. I am so lucky that you can do two things at once and that you can repeat my words to me like that."

So I tried to become a better listener and focus my attention on her as she spoke. When we were first married, it took Herculean effort for me to not look at the mail when I walked in our house at night (a well-ingrained habit during my years as a single adult). Instead, I strove to ignore the mail and focus only on her. (The mail would call out to me the whole time, "Read me, read me, *read* me.")

Or I would mute the TV and turn toward her or put down a book for a moment. I tried to attend to her with my body language, listen to her, and then reflect what she said (what therapists call "active listening").

Problem solved, right?

Wrong. Amy often still didn't feel satisfied.

This was confusing to me because the marriage workshops, retreats, and books all said essentially the same thing: *a spouse needs to feel listened to*. Plus, the Bible talks a lot about listening. According to New Testament scholar Scot McKnight, the word *listen* appears over fifteen hundred times in the Bible, and the most frequent complaint in the Bible is that people don't listen. [2] In short, listening is really important in every relationship, including one's relationship with God.

In our marriage, though, active listening fell just a bit short of the target.

Then one day, after learning about the importance of emotions, the three streams of emotional insight, and the need to pray the Psalms emotionally, I finally discovered the missing ingredient in my listening attempts. I realized that it wasn't enough to listen well, and even not enough that she felt listened to.

"Amy, you don't want just to feel listened to," I blurted out. "You want to *feel felt*." [3]

"Yes, that's it!" she exclaimed.

This may be the single most important truth I have learned about marriage in all my years on planet Earth. Once this hit me, I saw instantly why all my previous "listening proofs" had fallen short. Repeating her words to her in no way communicated that I had caught what she was feeling as she expressed those words. In fact, my tone betrayed that I hadn't a clue what she was feeling.

Giving her my full attention and reflecting her words back to her also fell short. It wasn't enough for her to *know* that I *understood* her feelings, because both knowing and understanding are cognitive events. She needed to *feel* that I *cared* about her emotions. Listening to her on a head level was not clearing the bar; she needed me to engage with her on a heart level.

Like a person deprived of an essential vitamin, she was hungry for a better connection with her husband but couldn't pinpoint exactly what she was missing. Thank God that through therapy, study, and lots and lots of trial and error, we stumbled upon the grand solution. She was lacking experiences of close emotional connection with me. She was starving to feel felt by me.

I still mess up at this more than I succeed, but now I am trying to engage more with her emotions than merely her words. My goal is for her to *feel felt*, rather than simply *feel heard*, and her goal is the same toward me. It makes a huge difference for both of us. We are learning about our emotional lives at a deeper level than ever before, and we both feel—get this—better *cared for* by the other. Not only better listened to, but also better valued, better *loved*. And that's what marriage is all about.

Entrainment:

"Sensing what others feel without their saying so captures the essence of empathy. Others rarely tell us in words what they feel; instead they tell us in their tone of voice, facial expression, or other nonverbal ways...

"Partners adept at empathizing do something quite extraordinary physiologically. Their own body mimics their partner's while they empathize. If the heart rate of the partner...goes up, so does the heart rate of the partner who is empathizing; if the heart rate slows down, so does the heart rate of the empathic spouse. This mimicry involves a biological phenomenon called entrainment, a sort of intimate emotional tango."[4]—Daniel Goleman

Attunement

Biologists may speak of *entrainment*, but psychologists call this *attunement*: the ability to recognize the emotional states of others and then to respond to those feelings emotionally. Attunement is resonating with another person's feelings. It is joining the other on an emotional level and sharing the emotional experience.

Consider the example of a tuning fork. A piano tuner takes a high-quality tuning fork, usually pitched to A440, the A above middle C, and strikes it softly. She then plays the piano key that is supposed to produce the same note and listens to the two sounds. If they are out of tune and do not resonate, the tuner tightens or loosens the tension of that piano string until perfect resonance is achieved. When the tuning fork and the piano string produce sounds with exactly matching frequencies, they are said to be in tune or attuned.

In the same way, two people can be attuned emotionally. When one shares a joke and the other spontaneously laughs, the two are resonating on the same emotional frequency. However, if one shares a joke and the other doesn't laugh or crack a smile, there is a clear lack of attunement.

A more important example is when one person shares burdens or sorrows and a listening friend wells up in tears. When this happens, deep emotional resonance is taking place. The person who shared feels felt by the other emotionally. The opposite is also true. Real emotional dissonance occurs if a deeply grievous experience is shared and the listening friend shows no emotional reaction. The sharing friend may know that she was listened to, but will not feel felt.

Of course, I am not suggesting that we should laugh if we don't think a joke is funny or manufacture tears if we don't feel sad. Emotions are not something that should be staged or spun.

Instead, as we listen to another person, we can do what we do as we pray the Psalms. We begin by paying attention to the person's emotions as they are expressed both verbally and physically. Then, when the appropriate moment for us to respond arrives, we reflect not just the facts heard, but instead we focus on the feelings. In praying the Psalms we have learned to focus on the emotions in the text and then ask God, "Why did you bring up this emotion today? Is there something here that we should talk about? What are you feeling that I need to feel with you?" We essentially can do so in our human relationships as well.

Picture it this way: in relationships we try to match the other's emotional frequency, like tuning in a radio station in the days before digital radios. To find a station we had to "tune in" the signal. By turning the frequency dial slowly, back and forth, we found the spot with the best sound. In relationships, we do a similar thing. We try to locate the emotional frequency of a loved one, which also takes trial and error.

A child may come home from school in a grumpy mood. Some parents might say, "Stop being a grump and put on a happy face," which usually means the kid gets grumpier. This is because "Stop being a grump and put on a happy face" denies the child's emotions, misses the attunement opportunity, and actually creates a larger emotional chasm. Additionally, on a pragmatic level, it squanders the chance to discover important events that might have happened to the child that day, events that might have put the child at risk.

An emotionally healthy parent will notice the emotion and gently try to turn the dial to find out the source of the grumpiness. Unfortunately, many parents are not well trained in seeking emotional attunement, so their few attempts to find the source of the emotions fall short. If the parent says, "What happened at school today?" many kids (especially teenagers) will respond, "Nothing." If the parent asks, "How did you feel at school today?" the response may be the same.

This is like static on a radio—clearly the station is not tuned in. So we parents begin to move the dial ever so slightly, back and forth, until we hear the beginnings of a signal. We might say, "How were your teachers today?" or "Did you do anything interesting in your classes today?" Still nothing but small talk and static. So we move the dial again: "How about the other kids in your class—how were they today?" Suddenly, bingo! We have hit the station and a clear signal comes in. "They were okay. Except for David, the big kid. He's a bully."

Now we are on to something, but we have to move the dial ever so gently or we will lose the signal. "Wow. Bullies can be really tough to deal with. Did David bully someone at school today?" We are gently moving the emotional dial, trying to get to the heart of the matter.

When children come home in a grumpy mood, they are unconsciously revealing important information about their day and teeing up the ball for us. They are saying, "Something hurtful happened to me today. Do you care?" They are giving us a grand opportunity to enter their world and learn about what is troubling them—which may even be a safety issue we really need to know about. A grumpy mood is a golden opportunity to explore and validate their feelings. They will probably never say this to us verbally, but their grumpiness is saying it nonverbally and unconsciously.

The same is true when a spouse comes home from work, when we talk to a friend on the phone, when we visit with others at church, or when we interact with coworkers at the office. If we notice the little emotional clues that are given and carefully tune the signal in more clearly, casual encounters can become significant ones. Helping others *feel felt* is an enormous advance in listening skills that can improve almost any relationship, and it is just one example of the benefits of growing toward emotional maturity. Emotional attunement is a powerful relational tool.

Jesus, the Master of Attunement:

After the death of Lazarus, Jesus traveled to Bethany, where Lazarus had lived with his sisters, Mary and Martha. As he neared the village, Jesus met Martha on the road first. She greeted him respectfully and offered a statement of faith, but never showed any emotion. Neither did Jesus.

When Mary met him, in contrast, she fell at his feet, offered the same profession, and wept. Others with her were also weeping. Jesus could have responded with a mild rebuke, "Dear friends, there is no need to weep. I am about to do an amazing miracle and bring Lazarus back to life. Wipe away those tears."

Instead, Jesus "was deeply moved in spirit and troubled" (John 11:33). Ken Hughes explains, "The word for 'was deeply moved' comes from an ancient Greek word that describes a horse snorting…it implies that our Lord let out an involuntary gasp. The wind just went out of him. E.V. Riev translates the thought, 'He gave way to such distress of spirit as to make His body tremble.'" [5]

Then, as it is recorded in the shortest verse in the Bible, "Jesus wept" (John 11:35). Concerning this verse, commentators often focus on Jesus' emotional openness and the raw humanity of Jesus that it reveals. Both are surely true.

But in the context of praying the Psalms, I am astounded at how deeply Mary and the mourners must have *felt felt* by

Jesus! How they must have felt his attunement with him. How wonderful that he paused to feel before he proceeded to heal.

Growing Closer to God

One day, as I was praying for God's help in my attempts to listen to my wife's feelings, it struck me that God has feelings too.

As we discussed earlier in this book, God—as revealed in the Bible—is clearly an emotional being. This is clear in the Psalms we will pray in this chapter. In Psalm 7 the psalmist says, "Rise up, O Lord, in your anger," and "God has indignation every day" (Psalm 7:6,11 nrsv). In Psalm 8, God "is mindful" and "cares" for us mortals, and has "crowned" us with "glory and honor" (Psalm 8:4-5 nrsv).

All of these are emotionally charged phrases about God's affective state. God is an emotional being, and the Psalms give us clues as to what those emotions are.

I began to think about the "Aha!" moment with my wife: how connecting with her on an emotional basis is what helps her feel loved and close to me. That is, she feels more loved and connected to me when she not only feels listened to but also feels felt.

So I wondered, does God feel emotionally listened to by me? *Does God feel felt by me when I pray?* Do I pause sufficiently when the Psalms provide glimpses into God's emotions and allow myself to feel those emotions with God? Then, do I communicate with God in a manner that would deepen our attachment connection? In short, do I attune with God in prayer?

Dan Allender and Tremper Longman III, in *The Cry of the Soul*, make a terrific suggestion about how such attunement with our own emotions better helps us to understand God's emotions:

> Our darker emotions reveal something—though in a skewed, bent, and tarnished way—about God's emotional life. How can we begin to understand the nature

of God's anger unless we enter into our own? How are we to gain any picture of what it means for a holy, righteous God to be jealous for His people if we ignore our human envy and jealousy? In the most peculiar fashion, He chooses to reveal His perfect heart by analogy with human emotion that is stained by depravity...The Psalms propel us into the deepest questions about ourselves, about others, and about God. As we let them expose the depths of our emotion, they will lead us to the God who reveals Himself in the midst of our struggle. [6]

Learning to Identify and Share What God Is Feeling

As we read the Psalms, we not only look for emotional clues that resonate with our emotional state or with the feelings of others, but we look for affective words and hints that reveal God's feelings. Yes, the Bible reveals that God not only knows all things, but he has specific feelings about events, people, and ourselves. We pray the Psalms from God's perspective, trying to learn not only from his knowledge but also his emotions. We pray in a manner so God will *feel felt*.

If this is a new concept for you, you are not alone. A few readers of early drafts of this book also struggled to grasp the idea that our prayers can affect how God feels. For some, the difficulty related back to the issue of the immutability of God—that God is perfect and thus cannot change—which we dealt with (and debunked) in an earlier chapter. Or some thought this implied emotional neediness on the part of God. This difficulty can easily be resolved: humans may need to feel felt by others, but that doesn't demand that God needs the same. In brief, God is not *needy* but surely *wants* to feel felt. As Richard Foster stressed, "We should always remember the words of Saint Augustine: 'God thirsts to be thirsted after.'" [7]

Others thought that any efforts on our part to make God feel felt smacked of works righteousness. This critique, as I see it, is similar to one commonly leveled against those who advocate drawing closer to God through spiritual formation. The critique is that efforts to draw close to God entail works righteousness. But effort does not imply works righteousness. As Dallas Willard pointed out in *The Great Omission*, "Grace is not opposed to effort, it is opposed to earning. Earning is an attitude. Effort is an action...Grace, you know, does not just have to do with forgiveness of sins alone." [8]

The key is the motivation behind the effort. If I try to help my wife feel felt because I want something from her, that is manipulation. But if I try because I want her to feel loved without any expectation of payback, that is love. Why would the same correspondence not apply to God?

Furthermore, the stupendous truth is that God is indeed moved by us, tiny humans that we are. He cares and is affected—literally—by our emotions. The Scripture reveals God as an emotionally responsive being who grieves, rejoices, thirsts, and loves. Our emotions affect God. As one early reader said to me, "For some bizarre reason, God is particularly fond of us and he wants us to learn to be particularly fond of him." As my wife and I desire to authentically feel felt by the other, God also desires—he *longs* for—the same with us. Jesus "*longed* to gather [Israel's] children together, as a hen gathers her chicks under her wings" (Luke 13:34), so why should we assume that God does not intensely desire to feel felt by us?

The God revealed in the Bible is a personal being with strong emotions. In Mark 8:12, Jesus "sighed deeply," which was clearly an emotional response. As I hinted at earlier, Psalm 7 contains at least two verses that reveal God's feelings:

> Arise, LORD, in your anger;
>   rise up against the rage of my enemies...
> God is a righteous judge,
>   a God who displays his wrath [indignation, NRSV] every day.
>   (Psalm 7:6,11)

Anger and indignation are strong emotions, and their presence in the Psalms is an intimate invitation into the heart of God. God is angry when his children are mistreated and when injustice is perpetrated. But rather than merely registering this on our cognitive clipboard, we can draw closer to God by praying about this emotionally.

> *Lord, your word reveals, right here in Psalm 7:6, that you are angry at the rage of my enemies. I've got to be honest—it feels so good to hear that. I've been burning with anger myself over their mean behavior, but I've also felt guilty about my anger, as if I were in the wrong for feeling mad. But since you have shared your feelings with me, I don't feel so alone anymore. And that makes me feel valued, stronger, and more secure. But most important, when you share with me what you feel, I feel closer to you.*
>
> *Lord, thank you for being mad at unrighteousness, and I ask you to rise up in your anger because:*

_____

_____

> *God, I thank you that you are a righteous judge, as you revealed in Psalm 7:11. I'm grateful that you are not a careless deity, like the pagan gods who are themselves unrighteous and immoral. Instead, you are righteous in your very core; purity and virtue are the essence of your being.*
>
> *And because you are righteous, you display your wrath "every day." To be honest, I've never thought about that before: that every single day, somewhere and somehow, you show your anger. You are not on the sidelines, unable to be involved until the game is over like the god of the deists. You are not waiting until our earthly lives are finished to judge and show your feelings about our*

behavior. The opposite is the case: "every day" you show your wrath.

Lord, the vast majority of humans are absolutely clueless about this. Many of them even have deluded themselves into believing that you are a deist God who is uninvolved or only a God of love who never feels or shows wrath. Of course, I know that you are a loving God also, but that does not negate or eclipse your wrath. You have revealed yourself as "the LORD, the LORD, the compassionate and gracious God, slow to anger, abounding in love and faithfulness" (Exodus 34:6). You have the capacity to be both loving and angry, and all the while completely pure and righteous. It's hard for me to fathom, but I accept it as true. I know in my heart it has to be true, otherwise you would not care when innocent people are hurt.

But you do care, Father, and you display your wrath every day. Give me eyes to see and a heart to discern this—especially when I am the one who has prompted your wrath. And help me to be able to understand your displays of wrath that are prompted by others, so I can better pray for them. But most of all, help me to discern your displays of wrath so I can understand your ways and your heart. I want to know you better and draw closer to you. Amen.

Learning to Share God's Positive Feelings

As we seek for God to feel felt as we pray the Psalms, it is natural to notice the negative emotions because they tend to burn with a brighter flame. But it is also helpful to be on the lookout for hints and clues as to God's positive emotions, though, like a gentle breeze, they may be more subtle and difficult to identify. A good example of that is found in Psalm 8:3-4,

> When I consider your heavens,
>   the work of your fingers,
> the moon and the stars,
>   which you have set into place,
> what is mankind that you are mindful of them,
>   human beings that you care for them?

This is a very clear pronouncement: God not only exists, but he cares. How different is this from the atheistic view of an uncaring universe! Carl Sagan, the science-worshipping secularist, said:

> Look again at that dot...The Earth is a very small stage
> in a vast cosmic arena...Our posturings, our imagined
> self-importance, the delusion that we have some priv-
> ileged position in the Universe, are challenged by this
> point of pale light. Our planet is a lonely speck in the
> great enveloping cosmic dark. In our obscurity, in all
> this vastness, there is no hint that help will come from
> elsewhere to save us from ourselves...The Earth is the
> only world known so far to harbor life. [9]

How surprised Sagan will be on judgment day to realize that he was completely, absolutely mistaken. Not about the vast size of the universe, mind you, nor the relative smallness of planet Earth. But he was dead wrong about life. Sure, there is life on Earth—which is no small miracle itself. But according to the Bible, the heavens and the earth are alive with supernatural beings, as well as infused with the very presence of the living God himself. There is more life in the universe than humans can ever comprehend. Furthermore, how shocked Sagan will be to discover that humans were never able to save themselves, but God did for us in Christ what we couldn't do for ourselves.

In like manner, Richard Dawkins, the virulent and vituperative proselytizer of atheism, wrote:

Nature is not cruel, pitiless, indifferent. This is one of the hardest lessons for humans to learn. We cannot admit that things might be neither good nor evil, neither cruel not kind, but simply callous—indifferent to all suffering, lacking in purpose. [10]

That's enough to depress anyone (and give logicians fits due to the clear contradiction: Is nature indifferent or not?). Fortunately, the Bible declares the opposite: the most foundational truth about reality and all existence is that God is real. Plus, this existent God is neither "indifferent to all suffering" nor "lacking in purpose." It is almost comical to me that Dawkins is so completely wrong, 180 degrees off target. He might as well have said, "Up is really down," or "Red is actually blue."

The psalmists knew better. God is both real and intensely involved with his creation—including human beings. He is both mindful of them and cares for them.

Which means that God cares about me, about you, and even about Carl Sagan and Richard Dawkins. God cares. Just think about that for a few moments. *Selah*. Meditate on this extremely rich morsel. God cares.

This is exactly what occurs in Psalm 8: the psalmist meditates on God's amazing governance of both the universe in its immensity and also of each human in our unique specificity. Pray this Psalm emotionally. Pray it aloud, circling every emotionally laden word or phrase and adding any notes or comments as to how it relates to your life. Then back up to its beginning and pray it again, in your own words, to your caring heavenly Father:

> Lord, our Lord,
>   how majestic is your name in all the earth!
> You have set your glory
>   in the heavens.
> Through the praise of children and infants

you have established a stronghold against your enemies,
    to silence the foe and the avenger.
When I consider your heavens,
    the work of your fingers,
the moon and the stars,
which you have set in place,
what is mankind that you are mindful of them,
    human beings that you care for them?
You have made them a little lower than the angels
    and crowned them with glory and honor.
You made them rulers over the works of your hands;
    you put everything under their feet:
all flocks and herds,
    and the animals of the wild,
the birds in the sky,
    and the fish in the sea,
    all that swim the paths of the seas.
LORD, our Lord,
    how majestic is your name in all the earth!
                              (Psalm 8:1-9)

Our Caring Heavenly Father

Care, of course, is an emotional word. *Webster's* gives six possible definitions:

1. Mental suffering; grief.

2. A burdensome sense of responsibility.

3. Painstaking or watchful attention; heed; caution.

4. A caring, or liking.

5. Charge, oversight, management, or custody.

6. A person or thing that is an object of care. [11]

Could it be that God actually feels as *Webster's* describes? Does the statement "God cares" entail that he experiences mental suffering and grief? Then, does he feel a burdensome sense of responsibility and painstaking attention? And does God take a liking to us, and even a liking to feeling this way?

Yes, it's all true. Secular philosophers may never arrive at these conclusions (maybe they are unaware of the importance of emotions to personhood), but the Bible reveals a God imbued with these qualities in the revelation of the Trinity—God as Father, Son, and Holy Spirit.

The Bible is not embarrassed about the emotions of God. It describes God the Father as sorry and deeply troubled during the time of Noah (Genesis 6:6), depicts the suffering of the Messiah Son (Isaiah 53:4; Hebrews 2:9), and tells us about the grief of the Holy Spirit (Isaiah 63:10; Ephesians 4:30). Furthermore, the Psalms reveal that God carries our burdens:

> Praise be to the Lord, to God our Savior,
>   who daily bears our burdens.
> (Psalm 68:19)

There it is again, dear reader: *daily*. Pause and drink this in. Our burdens are not ours to bear alone; God carries them every day. Hallelujah!

As we proceed through the Psalms, we will come upon many revelations of the emotions of God—which we can then use as opportunities to attune with God in prayer. One of my favorites is Psalm 133. It is found in the group of Psalms called the Songs of Ascent (120–134), and it has always been easy for me to pray when some relationship in my life goes awry. Let's read the Psalm, verse by verse, and pause to pray in such a manner that God will feel felt:

> How good and pleasant it is
>   when God's people live together in unity!
> (Psalm 133:1)

*Lord, you must love it when your people all get along
together! It's a good thing and it brings you pleasure. God,
I want my relationships to bring you pleasure, and it saddens me to think that it doesn't bring you pleasure when I
don't get along with others.*

*I know that right now my wife and I (or my parents and I,
my coworkers...my friends...my neighbors...) aren't getting along.*

*Lord, please forgive us when we let little things divide us.
Like right now, Lord, we are arguing about:*

_____

_____

*Lord, what are your thoughts about that? What would Jesus
do if he were in my place? Am I making too big a deal
about this? Is my ego getting in the way of our unity? Am
I sacrificing your pleasure on the altar of my pride?*

_____

*Lord, what can I do so that she (or he) and I can dwell in
true unity? (Selah: Pause, be quiet, and listen for God's
answer to that question. He will answer in his own time
and way. If God doesn't answer, move ahead but keep listening for his answer during the rest of the day.)*

_____

Now that you have prayed Psalm 133:1 about one relationship,
maybe there are others that also need this type of intercession. If this
is the case, you may want to repeat the prayer, pause and listen, and
then pray again for others with whom you are not at peace.

And Lord, I know that right now _____ and I

aren't getting along, Lord, please forgive us when we let
little things divide us...

After praying through Psalm 133:1, observe how the psalmist turns
to the benefits of unity. However, he expresses them in similes that
are difficult to understand for those of us who live far from the land
of Israel. So, before we pray, let's unpack their meaning.

> It is like precious oil poured on the head,
>   running down on the beard,
> running down on Aaron's beard,
>   down on the collar of his robe.
> It is as if the dew of Hermon
>   were falling on Mount Zion.
> For there the LORD bestows his blessing,
>   even life forevermore.
>   (Psalm 133:2-3)

The imagery of oil dripping off one's beard in verse 2 may not
sound attractive to modern ears, but in the psalmist's day it was a
symbol of abundance. In the arid climate of Israel, skin and hair
dried out quickly. For those who were wealthy enough to have an
abundance of olive oil, it was massaged into their scalps and faces for
medicinal reasons. In addition, the heads of priests (Aaron) were to
be anointed with sacred oil for ceremonial purposes (Exodus 30:22-
33). But in either case, to have so much oil poured on one's head that
it ran down the beard and onto the collar of one's robe was a sign of
extravagance and profligacy, of blessings beyond measure or imagina-
tion. In our culture, someone might say, "I am so blessed, I feel like
I won the lottery."

Verse 3 continues in the same vein with a different metaphor:
Mountain Dew! (Of course the psalmist is not referring to a twenti-
eth century drink, but I capitalized these words in honor of my sons,
who love the soda.) Israel is a seacoast Mediterranean country with a

flat topography. Jerusalem itself, though often referred to as Mount Zion, is really more of a hill than a mountain. As previously noted, the region is dry. While precipitation is extremely rare in Jerusalem in the summer, the wettest month, January, averages just five inches. Mount Hermon, on the other hand, is an actual mountain cluster that reaches over ninety-two hundred feet in elevation. The range straddles present-day Lebanon and Syria, just northeast of Israel. It is highly contested because of the great amount of rainfall and snow it receives. The runoff from Mount Hermon gives birth to streams and rivers, some of which eventually form the Jordan River.

Due to its elevation and moisture, Mount Herman can always be found, even in the summer months, to have generous morning dew on the ground. Imagine how the residents of Jerusalem, during the dry months, would dream of waking up to the plentiful dew they imagined to be present on Mount Herman. Thus, the psalmist writes, "It is as if the dew of Hermon were falling on Mount Zion." That is, unity is a wonderful and surprising event—like plentiful and free water in a desert. What a blessing that would be! For this reason, the Psalm ends with, "For there the LORD bestows his blessing, even life forevermore" (Psalm 133:3).

The blessing of unity and peacefulness is that wonderful—and it's a gift that God gives us not only now but also throughout eternity. Take a moment to pray Psalm 133 on your own. Whenever I do this, I am filled with a surprising sense of contentment and peace. Now that's something that should bring a smile to our faces and cause us to burst forth with thanksgiving.

Moving from Troubled to Thanksgiving Hearts

There is an added benefit to praying the Psalms. But before we turn to it, let's review what happens when we pray the Psalms:

- We discover that we are deeply loved and valued by God, the creator and sustainer of the universe.

- We learn that God is a personal God who not only has feelings but acts upon them.

- We gather that he desires that we bring our problems to him and entrust them into his hands.

- We learn that he wants to not only care for our needs but also to build close, emotionally satisfying relationships with us.

- We experience the surprising result: our entire perspective changes. Our problems become small as God becomes big. Our loneliness eases because God becomes personally and permanently present. Our burdens become lighter as we realize that he carries them—every day.

In addition to all of these wonderful results, when we pray the Psalms we arrive at this fabulous, surprising benefit of walking honestly and emotionally close with God: our mouths begin to bubble forth with praise, and our hearts, minds, and souls are filled with joy. As we pray the Psalms, we unearth one of eternity's greatest treasures: we learn to transform our worries into worship, which is the theme of the final chapter.

7

Moving from "Why God?" to Worship

The Psalms and the Transformed Christian Life

———— ✿ ————

"I go my way, and my left foot says 'Glory,' and my
right foot says 'Amen': in and out of Shadow Creek,
upstream and down, exultant, in a daze, dancing, to
the twin silver trumpets of praise." [1] —Annie Dillard

I will give thanks to the LORD with my whole heart;
   I will tell of all your wonderful deeds.
I will be glad and exult in you;
   I will sing praise to your name, O Most High.
            (Psalm 9:1-2 NRSV)

Why, O LORD, do you stand far off?
   Why do you hide yourself in times of trouble?…
The LORD is king forever and ever.
            (Psalm 10:1,16 NRSV)

One of the most remarkable qualities of the psalmists is their ability to move from weeping to rejoicing, from despair to praise. In a world filled with trouble, they were able to find peace. Even with their own hearts tortured by questions, they were able to worship. As Thomas Merton wrote,

If the Psalms are sometimes anguished, sometimes tormented, turbulent, warlike, defiant, yet they all end in peace, or show us that the way to peace is in confidence in the Strong Living God who is far above the struggles and tempests of earth, and who, nevertheless, descends on the wings of the whirlwind to rescue His elect…There is therefore one fundamental religious experience which the Psalms can all teach us: *the peace that comes from submission to God's will and from perfect confidence in Him.* [2]

This is clear in most of the Psalms: no matter how terrible the troubles nor how pressing the fears, they somehow turn, in the end, into praise. It is extremely rare that a Psalm, such as Psalm 88 that never utters a word of hope or praise, doesn't include an upbeat note.

More Precious than Gold—Much Pure Gold

As we pray the Psalms, we unearth and claim one of eternity's greatest treasures: we learn how to transform our worries into worship and our complaints into thanksgiving.

Though we are still in the beginning stages of praying the Psalms (after praying Psalm 9 and 10 in this chapter, we have 140 more to pray through on our own), we have uncovered the crucial key that unlocks God's power during times of trouble. We have hit ultra-valuable ore, the mother lode. We have uncovered secrets that are:

> …more precious than gold,
>   than much pure gold;
> they are sweeter than honey,
>   than honey from the honeycomb.
> By them your servant is warned;
>   in keeping them there is great reward.
>   (Psalm 19:10-11)

We have arrived at the purpose of prayer, the perfect end (*telos*) toward which the Psalms have all relentlessly pointed. After we face our emotions and get them all out on the table before God, something quite shocking happens: our distressing emotions, so horrifying in their intensity and debilitating power, become transformed. Our anger dissipates, our fear diminishes, and our worry disappears for a time. Gone. Poof. Vanished. We are made to "lie down in green pastures," are led "beside quiet waters," and find our souls "refreshed" (Psalm 23:2-3).

The Instant Benefit of Intimacy:

Johann Christian Arnold affirms the immediate, transformational power of relational closeness: "The positive results of sharing are often instantaneous: walls crumble as we realize that we are not alone in our feelings of isolation or guilt. Simply realizing that another person cares about our burdens can release us to see beyond them." [3]

As a result, our hearts are filled with a peace that "transcends all understanding" (Philippians 4:7).

What brings this peace that passes understanding, this transformational power that is more precious than much fine gold? It is not some mindset or ability of our own, not some higher stage of spiritual discipline that we have attained, as a Hindu guru finds an illusion of peace through severe disciplines of disengagement. No—rest for our souls is not a stage we reach, a prize we earn, or a commodity we can purchase. It is not an attainment, like another degree on a spiritual black belt. Contrary to almost everything else we do as humans, peace of mind is not something we do.

It's not about us at all. It's about God.

We find the deepest peace when we find closeness with God—that he is loving, trustworthy, all-powerful, and always present. We feel profoundly that we are his. Thus, we are assured of his protective care and that we are cradled in his caring arms. We feel deep attachment and attunement with God.

Peace is not a matter of whom we become but whose we become.

The secret to finding peace of mind, then, is learning how to experience God's closeness. It is a byproduct of not merely a cognitive belief in his immanence but an emotional awareness of his presence. After all, what we say we believe often doesn't align with what our bodies and emotions reveal that we believe.

The experience of emotional closeness with God is *transformational*. It changes us, including our attitudes and language. We swap our gripes for gratefulness; we go from worry to praise. A good example of this is Psalm 13:

> How long, O Lord? Will you forget me forever?
>   How long will you hide your face from me?
> How long must I bear pain in my soul,
>   and have sorrow in my heart all day long?
> How long shall my enemy be exalted over me?
> Consider and answer me, O Lord my God!
>   Give light to my eyes, or I will sleep the sleep of death,
> and my enemy will say, "I have prevailed";
>   my foes will rejoice because I am shaken.
> But I trusted in your steadfast love;
>   my heart shall rejoice in your salvation.
> I will sing to the Lord,
>   because he has dealt bountifully with me.
>   (Psalm 13:1-6 nrsv)

Though the author of Psalm 13 pours out his emotional pain and social distress to God, and though he asks God to hear and answer his call for help, there never is any hint that this prayer was answered. No clue that he was rescued. Yet the feeling of the nearness of God, reestablished through the psalmist's emotional praying, was sufficient to bring about a change of attitude. As a result, the psalmist abruptly switches from talking about pain and readies himself to rejoice and sing.

Martin Luther King Jr.:

During the Montgomery bus boycott of 1956, as Dr. Martin Luther King Jr. sat outside a courtroom during a noon recess, a reporter rushed toward him and said, "Here is the decision you have been waiting for. Read this release." Dr. King later wrote these words about his feelings on that eventful day:

"In anxiety and hope, I read these words, 'The United States Supreme Court today unanimously ruled bus segregation unconstitutional in Montgomery, Alabama.' My heart throbbed with an inexpressible joy. The darkest hour of our struggle had become the first hour of victory. Someone shouted from the back of the courtroom, 'God Almighty has spoken from Washington.'

"The dawn will come. Disappointment, sorrow, and despair are born at midnight, but morning follows. 'Weeping may remain for a night,' says the psalmist, 'but rejoicing comes in the morning.'" [4]

Yet another example is the prophetically astonishing Psalm 22. Here the psalmist catalogues a whole range of terrible troubles and woes:

My God, my God, why have you forsaken me?
    Why are you so far from saving me,
        so far from my cries of anguish?
My God, I cry out by day, but you do not answer,
    by night, but I find no rest...

But I am a worm and not a man,
   scorned by everyone, despised by the people…
I am poured out like water,
   and all my bones are out of joint.
My mouth is dried up like a potsherd,
   and my tongue sticks to the roof of my mouth;
   you lay me in the dust of death.
Dogs surround me,
   a pack of villains encircles me;
   they pierce my hands and my feet.
                    (Psalm 22:1-2,6,14-16)

This is both an agonizing situation in which the psalmist finds himself and an accurate foretelling of the suffering of Christ during the crucifixion. By quoting verse 1 on the cross, Jesus verified that this Psalm was a prophecy of the details of his own death. It is a horrific and excruciating account, and there is no verse that suggests that God rescued the psalmist and relieved his earthly suffering—which, of course, also was the case for Jesus.

Yet after expressing these painful emotions to God in prayer, the psalmist turns on a dime and begins to praise God—even while still suffering:

I will declare your name to my people;
   in the assembly I will praise you.
You who fear the LORD, praise him!
   All you descendants of Jacob, honor him!
   Revere him, all you descendants of Israel!
                    (Psalm 22:22-23)

These are amazing confessions of trust and praise amidst the psalmist's unceasing pain. And as the first words of Jesus on the cross exactly echoed Psalm 22:1, so too his later prayer, "Father, into your hands I commit my spirit" (Luke 23:46), expressed a level of trust similar to that of Psalm 22:22-23, though not a word-for-word citation. In Psalm 22, the psalmist models how we can move from anguished cries to trust-filled prayers, which Jesus perfectly modeled on the cross.

How does one move from worrying to worship, complaints to praise, or anguish to trust? Though this may sound simplistic, allow me to state the obvious: first we have to fully worry and complain and feel our anguish. We have to face our negative emotions head-on, allow ourselves to feel them, and bring those uncensored emotions before God in prayer. If we deny our worries, complaints, or questions, trying to swallow them whole, we will be unable to truly enter into worship. Like married couples who find the closest intimacy sometimes occurs after the most intense fights, so too the best worship may happen after difficult emotional honesty with God.

The Psalms usually follow this pattern: anguish or questions first, and then worship, thanksgiving, and trust follow. And the most common question in the Psalms is also probably the one each of us has uttered most often in our souls, "Why, God?" Psalm 22, as we saw just a few moments ago, begins with:

> My God, my God, why have you forsaken me?
>   Why are you so far from saving me,
>   so far from my cries of anguish?

Another example is found in Psalm 74, where the psalmist begins:

> O God, why have you rejected us forever?
>   Why does your anger smolder against the sheep of your
>   pasture?

In other words, before we can worship, we often have to ask "Why?"

We May Never Know Why

Cries of "Why, God?" are common on the lips of humans, even those who don't believe in God's existence. When a terrible tragedy befalls nonbelievers, suddenly they talk to the God they don't even believe in. They lament, "O God! Why is this happening?" or they swear and invoke God's name, which is coarsely similar to the curses in the imprecatory Psalms. Maybe their laments reveal a deeper theological awareness of God's presence than their rational minds can acknowledge. As I quoted earlier in this book, "The heart has reasons the mind knows not of." [5]

If nonbelievers cry out to God when suffering, it should be the case even more so for believers. The Psalms are proof of this, where we learn that it is okay to ask God "Why?"

In a time of distress, do you cry out to God, "Why?" I do quite often, and it is a wail I have heard many, many times from the lips of beloved church members. As a pastor, I often was speechless when I witnessed such disappointment with God. Here are just a few of the actual cries to God that I have overheard:

- "God—why aren't you answering our prayers for a job? Don't you care about the needs of our family?"

- "We prayed for a healthy baby. Why didn't you answer that prayer?"

- "Why did you let my marriage fail? I prayed for a miracle and didn't get it."

- "Why did you allow our church go through so much conflict and then a split? Don't you know how bad a witness this is to nonbelievers?"

Why? or Who?

William J. Peterson and Randy Peterson write in *The One Year Book of Psalms*: "Twice in the first verse of Psalm 10 the psalmist asks God *why*—a question the psalmists will cry out again and again throughout the Psalms. We may never find an answer to this question, but we can take great comfort in the answer to a

much more important question: Who? This is what the psalmist does at the end of this psalm. Once we catch a glimpse of
who God is, we can learn to trust him while his specific purposes remain hidden from us."[6]

The most anguished cries have come from those who have lost
loved ones to death (again, these are not invented instances):

- "Good Lord, why didn't you warn us that Grandpa had
  fallen into the pool? One little hint from you and we
  would have ran to save him. But you remained silent.
  Why?"

- "Why did you let him commit suicide? He believed in
  you, but when he needed you most, you let him take his
  own life. Why?"

- "Where were you, God, when our daughter was attacked
  and murdered? How could you sit quietly, up there in
  heaven, as she was treated so brutally? We just don't
  understand why you didn't raise a finger to help her."

The most riveting cries of all were from the parents who lost babies
or young children. Sudden and unexpected deaths brought about
some of the most spiritually challenging life events I've witnessed during my years as a pastor.

I still remember the repeated wails of a young mother at her child's
funeral. One of our church members had a coworker whose baby had
died from SIDS, and since they were not members of a church, they
had no one to speak at the funeral. My friends volunteered me.

A few days before the service, I met with the young father alone
since the mother was feeling sick that day. I gathered the information needed to conduct the funeral and tried to comfort him, but he
was very closed and stoic. Plus, I learned that he and his wife were
not interested in faith.

I prepared a eulogy and short message, and then went to the funeral home for the small service. I greeted the mother, who seemed barely able to stand on her own. She gave me no response at all—just silence and a vacant stare. The family and friends who gathered also seemed to be without faith, without comfort, and without hope. I prayed that God might use my feeble efforts to give them just a bit of all three.

But as I began the eulogy, the mother let out a loud, wailing cry: "God—why did you let our baby die?" The husband hugged her closely, trying to comfort her as best he could. I resumed the eulogy, and she seemed better for a short time, but then suddenly cried out again, "O God, O God—why did you let our baby die?" Other family members reached over to hold her hands or pat her back. She did this again and again, and during each wail I paused, tried to honor her sorrow, and then attempted to continue my message. But she continued, throughout the service, to erupt like an emotional volcano, spewing out the same fiery question: "Why, O God—why?"

Nothing I said brought any comfort or hope, and faith seemed insufficient to offer any solace to this family. They were all just spitting mad at God. I invited them to church to seek after the God who offers the hope of heaven and a reunion with lost children, but they just shook their heads in disinterest. They wanted their child alive now, not in some distant future.

Afterward, I felt like a failure. It was the most miserable funeral service in all my years of ministry.

I learned several lessons that day: (1) it is very difficult to comfort those who do not want to be comforted; (2) even people who don't believe in God get mad at him when they face intense suffering or injustice; and (3) I needed to pause and emotionally join people in their suffering before I had the right to offer comfort or theology. That day, though exceedingly difficult, better prepared me to handle future tragedies.

But the most important lesson I learned on that sorrow-filled day was this: it is impossible to answer the "Why?" questions people launch at God.

"The psalms are prayers of deeply religious men who are also profoundly puzzled, because the final explanation seems to slip through their fingers."—Stanley L. Jaki[7]

"The unanswerable 'Why?' is probably the hardest part of my job."—Jennifer Hoffman, MA, marriage and family therapist

This is certainly the case in the Psalms. The psalmists wail and complain and ask God "Why?" over and over and over. Sometimes, I even hear an echo of the voice of that inconsolable mother in the psalmists' laments.

Why is uttered thirty-three times in the Psalms, and two-thirds of them are addressed to God:

> Why, LORD, do you stand far off?
>   Why do you hide yourself in times of trouble?
>   (Psalm 10:1)

> I say to God my Rock,
>   "Why have you forgotten me?
> Why must I go about mourning,
>   oppressed by the enemy?"
>   (Psalm 42:9)

> You are God my stronghold.
>   Why have you rejected me?
> Why must I go about mourning,
>   oppressed by the enemy?
>   (Psalm 43:2)

> Awake, Lord! Why do you sleep?
>   Rouse yourself! Do not reject us forever.
> Why do you hide your face
>   and forget our misery and oppression?
>   (Psalm 44:23-24)

O God, why have you rejected us forever?
    Why does your anger smolder against the sheep of your
    pasture?…
Why do you hold back your hand, your right hand?
    Take it from the folds of your garment and destroy them!
                    (Psalm 74:1,11)

Though the psalmists repeatedly ask God "Why?" he never provides an answer. As God did with Job, he allows the question but does not offer any self-justification. Like a wise chaplain, God lets the psalmists express their confusion and pain, and he silently comforts them by the sheer reality of his presence. God suffers with them, shares their sorrows, and remains silent. He attunes with his anguished followers. God allows them to vent their grievous emotions and patiently listens to their questions—and even their attacks and slurs.

Yes, when we are in deep emotional pain, we sometimes say unkind things to those we love. "It's your fault that this happened." "I wish I had never met you." "I hate you." Out of our mouths flow caustic words and phrases, emotionally laden outbursts that we may later regret. But it feels good—doesn't it?—for a short time to vent a bit and release some of the emotional pressure that builds up inside. Those who love us know this, and even allow themselves to be emotional punching bags from time to time. (Of course, if one is treated as an emotional punching bag too often, it becomes abuse, which is not acceptable.)

God lets the psalmists verbally hit away at him; he can take it even when their comments are clearly undeserved. In one example, the psalmist compares God to a drunk who wakes up with a hangover: "Then the Lord awoke as from sleep, as a warrior wakes from the stupor of wine" (Psalm 78:65). In another Psalm, as Allender and Longman put it, God is "accused of being faithless—even a lousy businessman. 'You gave us up to be devoured like sheep and have scattered us among the nations,' he scolds God. 'You sold your people for a pittance, gaining nothing from their sale'" [8] (Psalm 44:11-12).

These are clear examples of emotion-based language, which would be construed as offensive outside the boundaries of deep relationships. But in relationships, they are acceptable when used in moderation. Yet many Christians never grant themselves the same privilege with God. They assume they must be holy and righteous when talking with a holy and righteous God—which is a joke in two respects. First, God knows they are neither holy nor righteous to begin with, so he sees right through this facade. Second, when they hide their true feelings from God and present a sanitized version of themselves to him, they are lying—which cancels any claim to holiness or righteousness.

Dear friend, God feels the anger in your heart before you are conscious of it, and he knows about your confusions and questions even before you can express them. "Before a word is on my tongue, you, LORD, know it completely" (Psalm 139:4). Hiding from God makes no sense at all, so go ahead and be honest with yourself and with him. Ask God your deepest questions; he already knows them anyway. Everyone suffers, so go to God with your hurts and sorrows. They are no surprise to him.

Only Empty Vessels Can Be Filled

After we fully and emotionally express our worries and complaints to God—which often form questions—we become empty and spent. Which is exactly where God wants us. As Mother Teresa said, "It is only when you realize your nothingness, your emptiness, that God can fill you with Himself." [9]

This is the consensus shared by saints, mystics, prophets, and Jesus himself: only empty vessels can be filled. For instance, St. John of the Cross, a sixteenth-century Christian mystic, wrote about the dark night of the soul. He said of the Christian who experiences emptiness: "When he is brought to nothing, the highest degree of humility, the spiritual union between his soul and God will be effected.

The journey does not consist on recreations, experiences and spiritual feelings, but in the living, sensory and spiritual, exterior and interior death of the cross." [10]

Isaiah, the eighth-century BC prophet, used other metaphors to express the notion that emptiness precedes filling: a farmer must clear the land before planting and the barren woman is most surprised when her womb is filled:

> "I will make rivers flow on barren heights,
>   and springs within the valleys.
> I will turn the desert into pools of water,
>   and the parched ground into springs."
>   (Isaiah 41:18)

> "Sing, barren woman,
>   you who never bore a child;
> burst into song, shout for joy,
>   you who were never in labor;
> because more are the children of the desolate woman
>   than of her who has a husband," says the LORD.
>   (Isaiah 54:1)

Most importantly, Jesus himself taught the same principle, expressed through the imageries of hunger, thirst, and sorrow:

> "Blessed are those who hunger and thirst for righteousness,
>   for they will be filled."
>   (Matthew 5:6)

> "Blessed are you who hunger now,
>   for you will be satisfied.
> Blessed are you who weep now,
>   for you will laugh."
>   (Luke 6:21)

And, finally, a psalmist hinted at God's use of the spiritual principle that emptiness comes before filling:

> You cleared the ground for it,
>   and it took root and filled the land.
>   (Psalm 80:9)

The conclusion is obvious: for those who have the spiritual wisdom to see through the pain of loss, emptiness can be seen as a herald of the fullness to come. Though we walk through dark valleys full of foes that surround us,

> You prepare a table before me
>   in the presence of my enemies,
> You anoint my head with oil;
>   my cup overflows.
>   (Psalm 23:5)

How can the psalmist feel safe when surrounded by enemies and be confident that God will fill empty cups to overflowing? The glorious answer is: a deep sense of God's close presence:

> Even though I walk
>   through the darkest valley,
> I will fear no evil,
>   for you are with me;
> your rod and your staff,
>   they comfort me.
>   (Psalm 23:4)

David finds comfort, even through times of sorrow and danger, not in answers to "Why?" questions or rational justifications for how God could allow bad things to happen to good people. He finds solace in God's company and strength in God's closeness: "You are with me." Because of this, he is filled with confidence even about the future:

Surely your goodness and love will follow me
    all the days of my life,
And I will dwell in the house of the LORD
    forever.

(Psalm 23:6)

Kathleen Norris on the Psalms:

I have found the reflections on the Psalms by Kathleen Norris to be very helpful. Here are a few nuggets that are deeply meaningful for me:

"The Psalms demand that we recognize that praise does not spring from a delusion that things are better than they are, but rather from the human capacity for joy."

"The great value of this songbook of the Bible lies not in the fact that singing praise can alleviate pain, but that the painful images we find there are essential for praise, that without them, praise is meaningless."

"The Psalms defeat our tendency to try to be holy without being human first."

"What the Psalms offer us is the possibility of transformation, of converting a potentially deadly force such as vengeance into something better." [11]

This is confidence in the face of danger, serenity in spite of circumstances, faith in the midst of trouble. Once we are absolutely, completely, 100 percent emotionally certain of God's love for us and presence with us, nothing can take away our security in God. He is the ultimate secure haven. As the apostle Paul wrote,

What, then, shall we say in response to these things? If God is for us, who can be against us? He who did not spare his own Son, but gave him up for us all—how will he not also, along with him, graciously give us all things? Who will bring any charge against those whom God has chosen? It is God who justifies. Who then is the one who condemns? No one. Christ Jesus who died—more than that, who was raised to life—is at the right hand of God and is also interceding for us. Who shall separate us from the love of Christ? Shall trouble or hardship or persecution or famine or nakedness or danger or sword? As it is written:

> "For your sake we face death all day long;
> we are considered as sheep to be slaughtered."

No, in all these things we are more than conquerors through him who loved us. For I am convinced that neither death nor life, neither angels nor demons, neither the present nor the future, nor any powers, neither height nor depth, nor anything else in all creation, will be able to separate us from the love of God that is in Christ Jesus our Lord (Roman 8:31-39).

In a virtuoso performance, Paul combines the four streams of emotional insight into a singular symphonic masterpiece:

- This is emotional intelligence: recognizing God's love for us, which conquers all.

- This is emotionally focused therapy and attachment language: though forces in this world attempt to separate us, we nonetheless have a secure haven in God. God is so strong, present, and reliable that nothing in all creation can separate us from the Father's care and protection.

- This is emotionally healthy spirituality: our fears, sorrows, and troubles are real, but also are rendered powerless by God's promises and presence.

- Finally, this is the essence of the psalmists' prayers: that God's presence and love are more certain and more determinative than any situation we might face.

With God close beside us, worries become worship and fears become praise. In Psalm 42 and 43, the author repeats the following phrase three times, which is why some medieval Hebrew manuscripts combine them into a solitary Psalm [12]:

> Why, my soul, are you downcast?
>   Why so disturbed within me?
> Put your hope in God,
>   for I will yet praise him,
>   my Savior and my God.
>
> (Psalm 42:5,11; 43:5)

This is a perfect example of the theme of this chapter. Our whys and worries are transformed, within a single verse, into hope and praise. But such emotional transformation is easier said than felt, so the author repeats it three times to cause it to sink in deeply, to move from his mind to his heart and ultimately into his very soul. Repetition helps with this process, which is why this is a beloved verse for many believers. Psalm 42:5 illustrates how a Psalm can begin so dark and turn so bright in the end, how fear turns into confidence and sorrows melt into serenity.

If you, dear reader, are often beset by worries and frequently find yourself downcast in heart and attitude, this verse is the perfect prescription. I recommend that you memorize Psalm 42:5 and pray it often. As was suggested in an earlier chapter, take a picture of it with your smartphone and make that photo your screen wallpaper. Write it on a sticky note and attach it to whatever you see often during your day: a computer screen, a delivery truck dashboard, or even a refrigerator door. Read it aloud and pray it often.

If you are a walker or runner, match each syllable of the verse with each step you take—sort of rap style. I have done this, and have occasionally been surprised to find myself repeating the words sub-vocally, though my mind was elsewhere. If you are musical, set this verse to a tune of your own creation. If you are not so gifted, replace the words of a well-known song with the words of Psalm 42:5. It can become the new chorus for a beloved hymn or new words for a soothing lullaby. I've memorized various things to the tunes of "Amazing Grace," "Baa, Baa, Black Sheep," and even "Pop Goes the Weasel" (I have no doubt your musical choices will be better than some of mine).

Let Your Feet Praise Him:

As quoted in the epigraph of this chapter, Annie Dillard ends her evocative *Pilgrim at Tinker Creek* with this delightful image: "And like Billy Bray I go my way, and my left foot says 'Glory,' and my right foot says 'Amen': in and out of Shadow Creek, upstream and down, exultant, in a daze, dancing, to the twin silver trumpets of praise."[13]

Give this a try next time you go for a walk or jog—you might find a reason to enjoy exercising. Rather than the army's "left, right, left…" march through life to the cadence of "glory, amen, glory…" or maybe "praise, worship, praise…" With one step say "*Hallelu*" and the next "*Yah.*" You can do this as you walk to work, amble toward your next class, or thread your way through the shopping aisles. After all, if the fields can "be jubilant," the forest can "sing for joy" (Psalm 96:12), and the trees can "clap their hands" (Isaiah 55:12), can't our walking feet proclaim his glory?

Praise and Thanksgiving as a Lifestyle

Imagine what life could be like if Psalm 42:5 became the defining theme of our lives—if we were able to always put our hope in God and praise him. As Augustine of Hippo said, "The Christian should be an alleluia from head to foot!"

Alleluia is the Latinized form of the Hebrew *hallelujah*, a word very prominent in the Psalms and especially so in the final five. I prefer to pronounce the word as "hallelu-YAH." This is because *hallelu* can be translated "praise" and *jah* is a shortened form of *Yahweh* (a form of the Hebrew, "I AM"). In English Bibles, *hallelujah* is most often translated "praise the LORD." The root *halal* (which means "to shine") is used over eighty times in the Psalms in this positive sense, most often translated as "praise" and a few times as "glory" or even "boast" (as "In God we make our boast all day long"—Psalm 44:8). [14]

In essence, praising God is wise because God himself is light and is the shining one, whereas praising ourselves is foolishness since we cannot generate light from within ourselves. We are like the moon compared to God's sun: God produces light within his own being, whereas we merely reflect his light and without it would live in utter darkness.

Since this is getting a bit technical, let me bring this back to our common lives with a true story. I was privileged to travel to India a few years ago and visit a mission sponsored by our church. Specifically, I wanted to see the orphanage that we had helped finance and meet the kids who were blessed to live there. All of them were beautiful beyond belief, and my heart was touched deeply that God allowed our church to be a big part of these kids' lives and salvation.

But there were two girls—twin sisters—that I will never forget because of their names: Praise and Worship. When I was introduced to them, I was speechless (a rare occasion for me)—the beauty and novelty of their names closed my mouth in awe. They were adorable little girls about six or seven years old, as cute as buttons, but it was the wisdom behind their names that floored me. To this day, they are my all-time favorite names.

Can you imagine the result of always saying "Praise" and "Worship" in day-to-day family life? "Praise, come to dinner." "Worship, have you brushed your teeth?" As a parent, I think these would be fantastic reminders to worship and praise God for his goodness throughout the day, and especially for his fabulous gift of children. And for the children themselves, their names have the power to shape their futures. I believe that Praise will grow to match her name and will become a woman adept at praising God and also praising (that is, encouraging) others. And Worship will grow to do the same. How could they not, given the reminders they hear every time their names are mentioned?

This is understandable even on a physiological level. Daniel Goleman points out that emotional intelligence can improve throughout our lives, especially through repetition. In order to replace old emotional habits (bad) with new ones (good), we must practice the better habit and inhibit the poor one. In Goleman's words, the result is that "the neural circuitry for the old behavior finally withers (psychologists call this extinguishing) and the circuitry for the better behavior grows stronger." [15] In other words, we can literally rewire our emotions—if we practice correctly and often enough.

Maybe this is one reason why God instructs us in the Bible to praise him, and also why churches gather every week for prayer and worship. Praising God over and over, week in and week out, contours our brains emotionally. We learn to be honest with God in prayer, and we habituate ourselves to connect closely with God in worship. Praise becomes a habit, and gladness and joy are the attendant emotions.

Your name probably is neither Praise nor Worship, but you can practice these emotional actions so often that they can become lifestyles for you—and shape your destiny in the process.

Augustine on the Psalms:

"St. Augustine adds that God has taught us to praise Him, in the Psalms, not in order that He may get something out of this praise, but in order that we may be made better by it. Praising God in the words of the Psalms, we can come to know Him better. Knowing Him better we love Him better.

Loving Him better we find our happiness in Him. 'Therefore, because He knew that this would be for our benefit, He made Himself more lovable to us by praising Himself.' These words [are] taken from St. Augustine's commentary on Psalm 144."
—Thomas Merton[16]

Worship Beyond the Pews

What would happen if Christians today chose to adopt the psalmists' lifestyles of praise and thanksgiving? If the attitudes of all Christians suddenly became dominated by worship and gratitude, maybe the world's opinion of us might improve. As G.K. Chesterton said, "The test of all happiness is gratitude." Building on Chesterton's comment, is it fair to say that the tests of true religion are gratitude and praise? Look at it this way: if our relationship with the God of love and glory doesn't cause us, his followers, to be filled with thankfulness and worship, something surely is wrong with our religion.

Though some books about the Psalms stress the negative genres of the Psalms (such as the Laments), the most frequent emotional word in the Psalms is a positive one: *praise*. It is used over two hundred times, and similar words (including *worship*, *thanksgiving*, and *rejoice*) occur an astonishing seven hundred times (see appendix 2, part 4).

So let's give praise and thanksgiving a try. Let's read a few Psalms, and then offer them as our own prayers.

In Psalm 9, David is in trouble and danger:

> LORD, see how my enemies persecute me!
>   Have mercy and lift me up from the gates of death.
>   (Psalm 9:13)

In a change of pace from the earlier Psalms, the author doesn't begin this Psalm with a complaint or worry. Instead, in a tremendous testimony to his close relationship with God, the psalmist is able to set aside his troubles and begin this Psalm with praise right out of the gate:

I will give thanks to you, Lord; with all my heart;
 I will tell of all your wonderful deeds.
I will be glad and rejoice in you;
 I will sing the praises of your name, O Most High.
(Psalm 9:1-2)

After a few verses in which the psalmist seems to gloat over the misfortunes of his enemies, he turns again to praising God for being a safe haven:

The Lord is a refuge for the oppressed,
 a stronghold in times of trouble.
Those who know your name trust in you,
 for you, Lord, have never forsaken those who seek you.
Sing the praises of the Lord, enthroned in Zion;
 proclaim among the nations what he has done…
Have mercy and lift me up from the gates of death,
that I may declare your praises
 in the gates of Daughter Zion
 and there rejoice in your salvation.
(Psalm 9:9-11,13b-14)

The psalmist begins with gratitude, and we are wise to do the same. In the words of William Arthur Ward, "God gave you a gift of 86,400 seconds today. Have you used one to say, 'Thank you'?" Let's use a bunch and try to make the psalmist's thanksgiving prayer our own:

I will give thanks to you, Lord, with all my heart;
 I will tell of all your wonderful deeds.

Lord, I want to pause and thank you from the bottom of my heart, for you have been wonderful to me and to others. So Lord, I thank you for:

_____

I thank you for:

_____

I thank you for:

_____

I thank you for:

_____

and I thank you for:

_____

I will be glad and rejoice in you;
    I will sing the praises of your name, O Most High.

> *Lord, just thinking about you and your attributes makes me
> smile, and fills my heart with happiness and joy.*
> *Your names, Yahweh (I AM), Yah-rophe (I AM who heals),
> Yah-yireh (I AM who provides), cause me to say Hallelu-
> Yah (praise I AM).*
> *So today I will sing and rejoice in your names. I praise you
> today because of who you are:*

_____

> *and because your names mean that:*

_____

_____

The LORD is a refuge for the oppressed,
    a stronghold in times of trouble.

Those who know your name trust in you,
for you, LORD, have never forsaken those who seek you.

> *So today I will sing and rejoice because you are my rock and
> my refuge. I praise you today because you are a safe haven
> for me.*
> *Unlike others who have left or abandoned me, you have
> promised, "Never will I leave you; never will I forsake
> you" (Hebrews 13:5). You are my strong tower, my safe
> place, my:*

_____

Sing the praises of the LORD, enthroned in Zion;
proclaim among the nations what he has done…
Have mercy and lift me up from the gates of death,
that I may declare your praises
in the gates of Daughter Zion
and there rejoice in your salvation.

> *So I will sing your praises today, and tell others of what
> you have done. I will tell of your goodness to these fam-
> ily members and friends, that they also will rejoice and
> praise you with me:*

_____

_____

Amen.

A Psychologist Comments on this Topic:

"Rick, I couldn't help but think about these concepts in terms
of Bob Emmons's research on gratitude. These findings mixed
with some of the findings from my current grace research

illustrate this principle: *happiness as a result of relational grati-tude*. This is illustrated in the Psalms by the call to…'Enter his gates with thanksgiving and his courts with praise; give thanks to him and praise his name' (Psalm 100:4). Here we are thank-ing Him for Him, not simple 'stuff.' This seems to me to be a 'relational thanksgiving'…which is what makes us 'happy/joy-ful.' The 'stuff' no longer fills us like it used to and is lacking in comparison to the happiness that comes from being loved by the Creator."—Kenneth A. Logan, PsyD, professor of coun-seling, Western Seminary, Portland, Oregon

A Life Filled with Love, Security, and Joy

Is such a life possible, even in the face of disappointments, trou-bles, and enemies?

The secular mind says no. It is impossible to be happy when hurt-ing, and it is unrealistic to always expect to be joyful. As Woody Allen wryly wrote in a fictitious commencement address, "More than at any other time in history, mankind faces a crossroads. One path leads to despair and utter hopelessness. The other, to total extinction. Let us pray we have the wisdom to choose correctly."

Secular pundits praised Allen's humor and honesty, while reli-gious commentators decried the nihilistic choice. But both missed the three most important words in the speech: Allen said, "Let us pray." (Actually, I think Allen missed their importance too.)

If only he had stopped there—he was so close to the real answer! His assessment of the paths facing mankind certainly seems valid in light of the mess we are making of our world. On our own, we face either despair or death. He's right.

But we are not alone. God is alive and well and still on his throne. He is neither dead nor asleep (Psalm 53:1; 121:3). What the world needs most are people who know this and pray.

So I return to our final question: Is it possible to live a life filled with love, security, and joy in a world filled with hopelessness and despair? The psalmists certainly thought so, as did the Hebrew worshipping community for whom these Psalms were compiled, and as do thousands of Christians who pray the Psalms each and every day.

The Art of Soothing Oneself:

"Downs as well as ups spice life, but need to be in balance. In the calculus of the heart it is the ratio of positive to negative emotions that determines the sense of well-being—at least that is the verdict from studies of mood in which hundreds of men and women have carried beepers that reminded them at random times to record their emotions at that moment. It is not that people need to avoid unpleasant feelings to feel content, but rather that stormy feelings not go unchecked, displacing all pleasant moods…The art of soothing oneself is a fundamental life skill."—Daniel Goleman[17]

One suggestion offered by Goleman to improve our sense of well-being is to capture hostile and cynical thoughts by writing them down[18]—which, it strikes me, is just what the psalmists did.

The remedy for our sickness is prayer: gut-honest, emotional, vulnerable prayer. And this is just what we find in the Psalms. As we join the psalmists by emotionally praying the Psalms daily, we find a better path, a different option that eluded Allen. It truly is the road less traveled. It is a lifestyle based on emotional prayer, which draws us close to God, and is modeled in the Psalms. In appendix 1, I provide a few pages to help you begin your journey of prayer through the Psalms. It leads to a life filled with love, security, and joy. Why would anyone choose another path when we can experience what the author of Psalm 46 found to be true? There really is hope for fear-ridden people and our war-torn world, and it is experienced when we draw emotionally close to God himself:

> God is our refuge and strength,
>   an ever-present help in trouble.
> Therefore we will not fear, though the earth give way
>   and the mountains fall into the heart of the sea,
> though its waters roar and foam
>   and the mountains quake with their surging. *Selah*.
> There is a river whose streams make glad the city of God,
>   the holy place where the Most High dwells.
> God is within her, she will not fall;
>   God will help her at break of day.
> Nations are in uproar, kingdoms fall;
>   he lifts his voice, the earth melts.
> The LORD Almighty is with us;
>   the God of Jacob is our fortress. *Selah*.
> Come and see the works of the LORD,
>   the desolations he has brought on the earth.
> He makes wars cease to the ends of the earth;
>   he breaks the bow and shatters the spear;
>   he burns the shields with fire.
> "Be still, and know that I am God;
>   I will be exalted among the nations,
>   I will be exalted in the earth."
> The LORD Almighty is with us;
>   the God of Jacob is our fortress. *Selah*.
>   (Psalm 46:1-11 NIV 1984)

A Closing, Magnificent Crescendo

Not only do many of the Psalms, often in the final verses, move from pain to praise and from complaining to thanksgiving, but the whole book of Psalms also does the same. The final third of the Psalms,

100 through 150, are filled with praise, and the last five are veritable *Hallelu-Yah* choruses—they begin with praise, are filled with praise, and end with praise. All five begin with "Praise the LORD" and end with "Praise the LORD," both translations of *Hallelu-Yah* in Hebrew. But the final prayer, Psalm 150, declares *Hallelu-Yah, Hallelu-El* ("Praise God"), *Hallelu-hu* ("Praise him"), or *Hallel* a total of thirteen times in six short verses. It's a downpour of praise, a cloudburst of worship:

> Praise the LORD.
> Praise God in his sanctuary;
>   praise him in his mighty heavens.
> Praise him for his acts of power;
>   praise him for his surpassing greatness.
> Praise him with the sounding of the trumpet,
>   praise him with the harp and lyre,
> praise him with timbrel and dancing,
>   praise him with the strings and pipe,
> praise him with the clash of cymbals,
>   praise him with resounding cymbals.
> Let everything that has breath praise the LORD.
> Praise the LORD.
>   (Psalm 150:1-6)

This is the result of a life spent walking honestly and emotionally close with God. His secure presence fills us with peace and, as a result, our hearts, minds, and souls begin to bubble forth with joyous praise.

How can we do this today? Not many of us have timbrels and cymbals ready at hand. What do we have today that can become places and ways we pour out our praise? Since over a billion people are users of social media, maybe this will work:

> *Hallelu-Yah!*
> *I praise you Lord, the great I AM,*

I praise you on my Facebook page,
  I praise you on Twitter.
I praise you on Instagram,
  and I praise you on Snapchat.
I praise you through email,
  and praise you with the occasional snail mail.
Let everyone who has access to social media
  praise the Lord! Hallelu-Yah!

Or we may prefer to praise him wordlessly. Francis of Assisi once said, "Preach the gospel at all times; if necessary, use words." This implies that we are perfectly able to preach wordlessly—and often probably do so unconsciously. Maybe we could express a lifestyle of praise and worship this way:

Hallelu-Yah!
  I praise you Lord, the great I AM,
  for you are a shield about me,
  and the lifter of my face (Psalm 3:3).
So today I will praise you with my smile,
  and glorify you with laughter.
I will praise you with happiness in my eyes,
  and joy emanating from my skin.
I will praise you with a countenance filled with gladness,
  and honor you with a visage of cheerfulness.
I will praise you by walking with light steps,
  and worship you by stepping along today's path cheerfully.
  Amen.

And as a last resort, we can always praise him the old-fashioned way—with words:

Hallelu-Yah!
  I praise you Lord, the great I AM,
  People will look at me today and wonder,

"Why is he so happy? Did he win the lottery or
    what?"
And I will answer, "I am happy because I am God's.
    I know I am loved and that fills me with joy."
So, dear Father, I will praise you by saying,
    "With God as my rock and my fortress,
    I have a secure haven and my safe place.
With him beside me and before me,
    what is there to fear or dread?
With him within me,
    what is there to worry or fret about?
That's why I'm happy;
    That's why I am so blessed!"
Praise the Lord! Hallelu-Yah!

APPENDIX 1

Praying the Psalms—
The First Days of Your Journey

This guide is provided as a template to help you begin praying the Psalms emotionally. You can use these pages to help you pray through the first three Psalms, after which you can follow the same procedures in a journal or notebook. As you begin, I suggest that each day you go through the four simple steps discussed in chapter 1:

Step One: Read the Psalm aloud, marking as you go each emotionally laden word or phrase with a pencil or highlighter (and remember to read with passion, as if you are an actor on a stage). For instance, in Psalm 4:1 (NKJV), your highlights might look like this:

> Answer me when I call, O God of my right!
> You gave me room when I was in distress.
> Be gracious to me, and hear my prayer.

Step Two: On the blanks provided below, write the emotional words or phrases you have marked. In Psalm 4:1, you may fill in the first few blanks like this:

Answer   I call   distress

Step Three: Look again, closely and prayerfully, at each word or phrase you have written on the blanks. Do any of the emotions relate to a situation you are going through right now or a feeling you are experiencing? Feel free to write any correspondences next to the emotional words. (I like to put stars next to the ones that really hit a nerve.) If some words remind me of what a friend or family member is going through, I note that as well. In Psalm 4:1, the annotations could look like this:

Answer me	I call	distress
(I need more than listening)	(like a fearful child to a parent)	(This is exactly how I feel!)

Step Four: Finally, write a short prayer, in the space provided, based on the emotional words you have annotated. Then pray your emotionally personalized Psalm aloud, filling in whatever words or phrases are needed, as I have modeled throughout this book. I prefer to pray orally rather than write out a prayer. However, because writing helps prevent mental wandering as we pray, I strongly recommend that you write your prayers for the first week. Psalm 4:1 may end up like this:

> Lord, I know that you are listening to me, since you know all things and listen to everyone. But I need more than just listening from you—I need answers! I cry out to you, like young, fearful children cry out to their parents. They cry out because they are in distress—which is exactly how I am feeling. Yesterday a very distressing thing happened. I want to tell you about it, and I need some answers about how I should respond. Maybe the answers will be in this Psalm today! Anyway, this is what happened...

When I pray the Psalms emotionally, I sometimes make it through only a few verses. In that case, I just mark the place in my journal and return to it the next day.

In this appendix I've provided the Scriptures, blanks, and prayer space to begin your prayer journey. You may want to copy these pages, along with your answers, into a blank journal, which you can then use with the rest of the Psalms. In time, you will fill many journals that will become records of your journey into closeness with God. Bon voyage!

DAY ONE—Psalm 1 (NRSV)

Step One: Read this Psalm aloud, highlighting any emotional words or phrases:

> ¹ Happy are those
>   who do not follow the advice of the wicked,
> or take the path that sinners tread,
>   or sit in the seat of scoffers;
> ² but their delight is in the law of the LORD,
>   and on his law they meditate day and night.
> ³ They are like trees
>   planted by streams of water,
> which yield their fruit in its season,
>   and their leaves do not wither.
> In all that they do, they prosper.
> ⁴ The wicked are not so,
>   but are like chaff that the wind drives away.
> ⁵ Therefore the wicked will not stand in the judgment,
>   nor sinners in the congregation of the righteous;
> ⁶ for the LORD watches over the way of the righteous,
>   but the way of the wicked will perish.

Step Two: On the blanks provided, write each emotional word or phrase you highlighted above:

Step Three: Prayerfully reflect on each of the emotional words that you listed in the previous step, and add comments next to those words as to how they relate to your daily life or to the lives of those you love.

Step Four: Weave the emotional words and comments into a prayer to your heavenly Father, who longs to connect and attune with you on an emotional level:

DAY TWO—Psalm 2 (NRSV)

Step One: Read this Psalm aloud, highlighting any emotional words or phrases:

¹ Why do the nations conspire,
    and the peoples plot in vain?
² The kings of the earth set themselves,
    and the rulers take counsel together,
    against the LORD and his anointed, saying,
³ "Let us burst their bonds asunder,
    and cast their cords from us."
⁴ He who sits in the heavens laughs;
    the LORD has them in derision.
⁵ Then he will speak to them in his wrath,
    and terrify them in his fury, saying,
⁶ "I have set my king on Zion, my holy hill."
⁷ I will tell of the decree of the LORD:
He said to me, "You are my son;
    today I have begotten you.
⁸ Ask of me, and I will make the nations your heritage,
    and the ends of the earth your possession.
⁹ You shall break them with a rod of iron,
    and dash them in pieces like a potter's vessel."
¹⁰ Now therefore, O kings, be wise;
be warned, O rulers of the earth.
¹¹ Serve the LORD with fear,
    with trembling ¹²kiss his feet,
or he will be angry, and you will perish in the way;
    for his wrath is quickly kindled.
Happy are all who take refuge in him.

Step Two: On the blanks provided, write each emotional word or phrase you highlighted above:

_____   _____   _____

_____   _____   _____

_____   _____   _____

_____   _____   _____

_____   _____   _____

_____   _____   _____

Step Three: Prayerfully reflect on each of the emotional words that you listed in the previous step, and add comments next to those words as to how they relate to your daily life or to the lives of those you love.

Step Four: Weave the emotional words and comments into a prayer to your heavenly Father, who longs to connect and attune with you on an emotional level:

DAY THREE—Psalm 3 (NRSV)

Step One: Read this Psalm aloud, highlighting any emotional words or phrases:

> *A Psalm of David, when he fled from his son Absalom.*
> [1] O LORD, how many are my foes!
> Many are rising against me;
> [2] many are saying to me,
> "There is no help for you in God." *Selah*
> [3] But you, O LORD, are a shield around me,
> my glory, and the one who lifts up my head.
> [4] I cry aloud to the LORD,
> and he answers me from his holy hill. *Selah*
> [5] I lie down and sleep;
> I wake again, for the LORD sustains me.
> [6] I am not afraid of ten thousands of people
> who have set themselves against me all around.
> [7] Rise up, O LORD!
> Deliver me, O my God!
> For you strike all my enemies on the cheek;
> you break the teeth of the wicked.
> [8] Deliverance belongs to the LORD;
> may your blessing be on your people! *Selah*

Step Two: On the blanks provided, write each emotional word or phrase you highlighted above:

_____ _____ _____

_____ _____ _____

_____ _____ _____

_____ _____ _____

_____ _____ _____

_____ _____ _____

Step Three: Prayerfully reflect on each of the emotional words that you listed in the previous step, and add comments next to those words as to how they relate to your daily life or to the lives of those you love.

Step Four: Weave the emotional words and comments into a prayer to your heavenly Father, who longs to connect and attune with you on an emotional level:

APPENDIX 2

Lists of Emotional Words in the Psalms

1. Alphabetical List of Emotional Words in the Psalms (NIV)

A

Abandon	2	Afraid	5	Ashamed	1
Abandoned	1	Agony	2	Assail	1
Abhor	1	Alarm	1	Astounded	1
Abhorred	1	Alliance	1	Astray	1
Abounding	1	Aloof	1	Attentive	2
Abundance	4	Alter	1	Avenge	1
Abundant	3	Anger	28	Avenged	1
Abuse	1	Angered	2	Avenges	2
Acclaim	1	Angry	9	Awe	2
Accursed	1	Anguish	9	Awesome	12
Accusations	2	Anxiety	1		
Accuse	2	Anxious	1	**B**	
Accuser	1	Appalled	1	Beautiful	1
Accusers	3	Appeal	1	Beauty	2
Accusing	1	Aroused	2	Begging	1
Afflicted	20	Arrogance	3	Bereaved	1
Affliction	6	Arrogant	14	Betray	1
		Arrogantly	1	Betrayed	1
				Bitter	2

Blameless	14	Cherish	1	Contempt	8
Bless	16	Cherished	1	Content	1
Blessed	30	Clamor	1	Contrary	1
Blesses	5	Cling	1	Contrite	1
Blessing	7	Coiled	1	Controlled	1
Blessings	3	Collapse	1	Convulsed	1
Blighted	1	Comfort	6	Cordially	1
Bloodthirsty	4	Comforted	2	Corrupt	3
Boast	6	Comforters	1	Courage	1
Boastful	1	Commends	1	Cower	1
Boasting	1	Compassion	12	Craved	2
Boasts	1	Compassionate	5	Craving	1
Brightness	1	Complaint	2	Cravings	1
Broke	1	Conceal	1	Cried	12
Broken	4	Concern	1	Cries	3
Brokenhearted	3	Concerned	1	Cringe	2
Brute	1	Condemn	3	Crooked	1
Burden	2	Condemned	4	Cruel	2
Burned	1	Confess	1	Crush	1
		Confidence	1	Crushed	6
C		Confident	1	Crushing	1
Calamity	1	Confined	1	Cry	36
Callous	3	Confound	1	Cunning	2
Calm	1	Confronted	1	Curse	3
Calmed	1	Confuse	1	Cursing	1
Care	2	Confusion	4		
Careful	1	Conspiracy	1	**D**	
Cares	2	Conspire	7	Dancing	1
Celebrate	2	Consumed	3	Dark	3
Chastened	1	Consumes	1	Darkened	1

Darkest	2	Destroy	1	Dread	5
Darkness	17	Destroyed	11	Dreamed	1
Dashed	1	Destroying	2	Dwells	1
Decay	3	Destroys	1		
Deceit	4	Destructive	1	**E**	
Deceitful	14	Detest	2	Eagerly	1
Deception	1	Devastated	2	Embittered	1
Deep	2	Devious	1	Emboldened	1
Defiantly	1	Devise	6	Encourage	2
Defiled	4	Devised	1	Endowed	1
Delight	24	Devour	3	Endure	8
Delighted	1	Devoured	2	Endured	2
Delightful	1	Devours	1	Endures	45
Delights	5	Discern	2	Engulf	1
Delusions	1	Discernment	1	Enjoy	2
Demanding	1	Discipline	1	Enrich	1
Deprived	1	Disgrace	10	Ensnared	1
Depths	3	Disgraced	3	Entangled	2
Derision	3	Disillusionment	1	Enthralled	1
Desecrated	1	Disloyal	1	Entrust	1
Desire	10	Dismay	1	Envied	1
Desired	2	Dismayed	3	Envious	2
Desires	5	Displeasure	1	Envy	1
Desolations	1	Distraught	1	Exalt	12
Despair	2	Distress	21	Exalted	24
Desperate	3	Disturbed	3	Exalts	1
Despise	4	Doomed	1	Excellent	1
Despised	6	Double-minded	1	Expound	1
Despises	1	Downcast	4	Extol	10
Destitute	1	Drawn	1		

F

Fade	1	Forget	2	Glory	38
Fail	3	Forgiven	1	Gnashed	1
Failed	1	Forgiveness	1	Good	37
Fails	3	Forgives	1	Goodness	7
Faints	7	Forgiving	2	Grace	1
Falsehood	1	Forgotten	4	Gracious	10
Falsely	1	Forsake	6	Grateful	1
Faltered	2	Forsaken	5	Great	24
Fantasies	1	Free	1	Greater	1
Fate	1	Freed	1	Greatness	2
Favor	6	Freedom	1	Greedy	1
Favored	1	Fret	3	Grief	4
Fear	49	Frustrate	1	Grieved	2
Feared	7	Frustrates	1	Groan	3
Fearfully	1	Fulfill	2	Groaned	1
Fears	2	Fulfills	1	Groaning	3
Feeble	1	Furious	3	Groans	2
Fester	1	Futile	1	Grow	2
Festive	1	Futility	2	Grumbled	1
Fierce	2			Guilt	5
Flatter	3	**G**		Guilty	2
Flattering	1	Generosity	1		
Flee	1	Generous	2	**H**	
Flourish	7	Glad	22	Happy	4
Flourishing	1	Gladdens	1	Harbor	1
Folly	2	Gladness	5	Harden	1
Foolish	2	Glee	1	Harm	4
Fools	3	Gloat	7	Harness	1
Forgave	3	Glorify	4	Hate	22
		Glorious	5	Hates	1

Hatred	3	Injustice	2	Lights	1
Haughty	3	Innocence	2	Loathed	1
Healed	2	Innocent	2	Loathing	1
Heals	2	Insight	1	Loathsome	1
Healthy	1	Insulting	1	Lofty	1
Heat	1	Integrity	3	Lonely	2
Help	6			Longing	3
Helpless	4	**J**		Longings	2
Hidden	1	Jealousy	2	Longs	1
Honor	10	Joy	52	Love	138
Honored	2	Joyful	2	Loved	4
Honors	1	Joyfully	2	Lovely	1
Hope	34	Jubilant	3	Loves	9
Hopes	2	Just	3	Loving	4
Horror	1	Justice	13	Low	1
Hostility	1	Justly	2	Lowly	1
Hot	1			Loyal	3
Hotly	1	**K**		Lurk	1
Howl	1	Kindly	1	Luxuriant	1
Humble	4	Kindness	4	Lying	1
Humbled	5	Knowledge	1		
Humility	1			**M**	
Hurts	1	**L**		Majestic	5
Hypocrites	1	Lack	1	Majesty	7
		Lament	1	Malice	5
I		Laugh	4	Malicious	1
Ignorant	1	Laughs	1	Maliciously	2
Indignation	3	Laughter	1	Malign	1
Iniquities	2	Leaning	1	Marvelous	5
Iniquity	4	Lies	1	Meek	1
		Light	18		

Merciful	7	Overtaken	1	Plots	2
Mercy	29	Overwhelmed	8	Plunder	1
Might	1			Plundered	1
Mighty	17	**P**		Poison	1
Miry	1	Pain	3	Ponder	3
Mischief	1	Pants	2	Poor	8
Misery	3	Partiality	1	Power	15
Misuse	1	Patiently	2	Powerful	1
Moan	1	Peace	15	Praise	201
Mock	5	Peaceably	1	Praised	2
Mocked	5	Perceive	1	Praises	16
Mockers	1	Perfection	1	Praiseworthy	1
Mourning	4	Perish	6	Praising	1
		Persecute	3	Precious	7
N		Persecuted	1	Preserve	8
Need	1	Perverse	1	Preserved	1
Needy	18	Pierce	1	Preserves	3
Neglect	1	Pierced	1	Pride	6
Noble	2	Pity	2	Proclaim	11
		Plagued	1	Profound	1
O		Plea	2	Promise	1
Oblivion	1	Plead	1	Promises	1
Offensive	1	Pleasant	5	Promised	1
Oppress	4	Please	2	Protect	4
Oppressed	10	Pleased	3	Protection	1
Oppression	5	Pleases	2	Protects	2
Oppressors	1	Pleasing	2	Proud	7
Overawed	1	Pleasure	3	Proudly	1
Overcome	3	Pleasures	1	Prowl	2
Overflows	1	Plot	7	Pure	7

Q

Quake	2
Quaked	2
Quaking	1
Quiet	2
Quieted	1

R

Radiant	4
Rage	1
Rages	1
Rash	1
Ravages	1
Rebelled	7
Rebelling	2
Rebellious	5
Rebuke	7
Rebuked	3
Rebuking	1
Reduced	1
Reeled	1
Refreshed	1
Refreshes	1
Refreshing	1
Refuge	20
Regard	2
Reject	8
Rejected	12
Rejoice	35
Rejoiced	1

Rejoices	6
Rejoicing	3
Relent	1
Reliance	1
Relied	1
Relief	2
Rely	1
Remember	2
Remembered	1
Renew	1
Renewed	1
Renounced	1
Renown	1
Reproach	2
Repulsive	1
Rescue	3
Resound	1
Rest	5
Resting	1
Restore	4
Restores	2
Restrained	1
Revealed	1
Revenge	1
Revere	3
Reverence	2
Revile	3
Reviled	1
Reviles	1
Revive	2

Ridicule	1
Right	1
Roared	1
Roaring	2
Rouse	1
Ruin	4
Ruthless	4

S

Safe	3
Safely	1
Sapped	1
Satisfied	6
Satisfies	3
Satisfy	5
Scattered	1
Scheme	1
Schemes	1
Scoff	3
Scorch	2
Scorn	11
Scorned	3
Scourge	1
Secure	6
Security	1
Seek	2
Self-denial	1
Selfish	1
Senseless	4
Shake	1

Shaken	12	Splendor	16	Sympathy	1
Shakes	2	Spurned	1	**T**	
Shame	43	Stagger	1		
Shamed	1	Staggered	1	Taunt	2
Sharp	1	Steadfast	6	Taunts	4
Sharpen	1	Stirred	1	Tears	7
Shattered	1	Storm	1	Tempest	3
Shield	1	Strayed	2	Terrified	2
Shine	9	Strengthen	1	Terrifies	1
Shines	2	Strengthens	1	Terrify	1
Shook	1	Strife	1	Terror	6
Shrewd	1	Strikes	1	Terrors	4
Sighing	1	Strong	6	Testify	2
Silence	2	Stronghold	2	Thanks	18
Silenced	3	Struggles	1	Thanksgiving	3
Silent	8	Stubborn	2	Thirst	2
Simple	1	Stumble	2	Thirsts	1
Slander	5	Stumbled	2	Threat	1
Slandered	1	Stumbling	1	Thundered	1
Slanders	2	Subdued	1	Thunders	2
Slimy	1	Subjected	1	Tolerate	1
Smeared	1	Success	1	Tottering	1
Smolder	1	Suffer	1	Trampled	1
Snare	1	Suffered	2	Treacherous	1
Snarling	2	Suffering	4	Treasured	1
Sneer	1	Surprise	1	Tremble	4
Sneers	1	Sustain	6	Trembled	2
Soften	1	Sustains	6	Trembles	4
Soothing	1	Swear	1	Trembling	3
Sorrow	7	Sweet	2	Tribute	1
Spew	1	Sweeter	2	Triumph	9

Trouble	22	**V**		Wholeheartedly	1
Troubled	3	Vain	6	Wicked	93
Troubles	8	Valiant	1	Wickedly	1
Trust	38	Vanish	1	Wickedness	7
Trusted	6	Vast	1	Willful	1
Trusting	1	Venom	2	Willing	1
Trusts	6	Vexed	1	Wisdom	5
Trustworthy	4	Victories	3	Wise	5
Truth	3	Victorious	1	Wisely	1
Turmoil	1	Victoriously	1	Wiser	1
		Victory	12	Wither	1
U		Violent	5	Withered	1
Unafraid	1	Vile	6	Withers	1
Understand	8	Vindicate	6	Woe	1
Understanding	14	Vindicated	1	Woes	1
Undivided	1	Vindicates	1	Wonderful	16
Unfailing	8	Vindication	4	Wonderfully	1
Unfaithful	1	Violate	2	Wonders	15
Unfeeling	1	Violates	1	Worn out	2
Unharmed	1	Violence	8	Worst	1
Unjust	1			Worthless	3
Unleashed	1	**W**		Wounded	1
Unmercifully	1	Wailing	1	Wrath	24
Unreliable	1	Wander	1	Wrestle	1
Untiring	1	Wayward	1	Writhed	1
Unwary	1	Weak	7	Wrong	10
Uphold	1	Weary	2	Wronging	1
Upholds	3	Weep	3		
Upright	19	Weeping	6	**XYZ**	
Uprightness	1	Well-nurtured	1	Yearns	1
Uproar	2	Wept	1	Zeal	2

2. List of Emotional Words Occurring Most Frequently in the Psalms (NIV)

Praise	201	Good	37	Great	24
Love	138	Cry	36	Wrath	24
Wicked	93	Rejoice	35	Glad	22
Joy	52	Hope	34	Hate	22
Fear	49	Blessed	30	Trouble	22
Endures	45	Mercy	29	Distress	21
Shame	43	Anger	28	Afflicted	20
Glory	38	Delight	24	Refuge	20
Trust	38	Exalted	24		

3. List of Grief-Related Emotional Words in the Psalms (NIV)

Abandon	2	Disillusionment	1	Sorrow	7
Abandoned	1	Distraught	1	Wailing	1
Afraid	5	Distress	21	Weep	3
Anguish	9	Downcast	4	Weeping	6
Anxiety	1	Grief	4	Wept	1
Anxious	1	Grieved	2	Woe	1
Bereaved	1	Groan	2	Woes	1
Broke	1	Groaned	1	**Total = 165**	
Broken	4	Groaning	3		
Brokenhearted	3	Misery	3		
Cried	12	Moan	1		
Cries	3	Mourning	4		
Cry	36	Shaken	12		
Despair	2	Shakes	2		
Devastated	2	Shattered	1		

4. List of Praise, Thanks, and Joy-Related Emotional Words in the Psalms (NIV)

Awe	2	Glorious	5	Rejoiced	1
Awesome	12	Glory	38	Rejoices	6
Beautiful	1	Gracious	10	Rejoicing	3
Beauty	2	Grateful	1	Shine	9
Bless	16	Happy	4	Shines	2
Blessed	30	Joy	52	Splendor	16
Blesses	5	Joyful	2	Thanks	18
Blessing	7	Joyfully	2	Thanksgiving	3
Blessings	3	Jubilant	3	Victories	3
Celebrate	2	Laugh	4	Victorious	1
Cherish	1	Laughs	1	Victoriously	1
Cherished	1	Laughter	1	Victory	12
Cordially	1	Marvelous	5	Wonderful	16
Dancing	1	Pleasant	5	Wonderfully	1
Delight	24	Please	2	Wonders	15
Delighted	1	Pleased	3		
Delightful	1	Pleases	2	**Total = 700**	
Delights	5	Pleasing	2		
Exalt	12	Pleasure	3		
Exalted	24	Pleasures	1		
Exalts	1	Praise	201		
Festive	1	Praised	2		
Glad	22	Praises	16		
Gladdens	1	Praiseworthy	1		
Gladness	5	Praising	1		
Glee	1	Radiant	4		
Glorify	4	Rejoice	36		

Notes

Chapter 1: Our Need for Emotional Closeness with God and Others

1. Eugene Peterson, *Answering God: The Psalms as Tools for Prayer* (New York: Harper-Collins, 1989), 101.

2. Robert C. Roberts, *Spirituality and Human Emotion* (Grand Rapids, MI: Wm. B. Eerdmans Publishing Co., 1982), 1.

3. Richard Foster, *Prayer: Finding the Heart's True Home* (San Francisco: HarperSan-Francisco, 1992), 13.

4. G.K. Chesterton, quoted in MaryKate Morse, *A Guidebook to Prayer: Twenty-Four Ways to Walk with God* (Downers Grove, IL: IVP Books, 2013), 13.

5. See Rick Stedman, *Praying the Promises of Jesus* (Eugene, OR: Harvest House Publishers, 2016), 41-47.

6. "If we could only see the heart of the Father, we would be drawn into praise and thanksgiving more often. It is easy for us to think that God is so majestic and so highly exalted that our adoration makes no difference to him. To be sure, the self-sufficiency of God is a precious doctrine, but we should always remember the words of Saint Augustine: 'God thirsts to be thirsted after.'" Foster, *Prayer*, 85.

7. Peter Scazzero, *Emotionally Healthy Spirituality* (Grand Rapids, MI: Zondervan, 2006), 124.

8. Jonathan Graf, *The Power of Personal Prayer: Learning to Pray with Faith and Purpose* (Colorado Springs, CO: NavPress, 2002), 104.

9. Beth Moore, *Praying God's Word: Breaking Free from Spiritual Strongholds* (Nashville, TN: Broadman and Holman Publishers, 2000), 6.

10. Quoted in Tremper Longman III, *How to Read the Psalms* (Downers Grove, IL: InterVarsity Press, 1988), 13. This is a terrific introduction to the Psalms, and each chapter provides a list of available resources for further study—except for the chapter about emotions and the Psalms, which makes this statement under the heading *Further Reading*: "Unfortunately, there is not much available on this aspect of the Psalms" (p. 85). It is my prayer that *Praying the Psalms* will fill this need.

11. Quoted in Longman, *How to Read the Psalms*, 85.

12. Brian J. Dodd, *Praying Jesus' Way: A Guide for Beginners and Veterans* (Downers Grove, IL: InterVarsity Press, 1997), 38.

13. Robert Warren, *The Practice of Prayer: A Companion Guide* (Grand Rapids, MI: Hamewith Books, 1994, 1998, 2001), 184-85.

14. Ray Stedman, *Talking with My Father: What Jesus Teaches Us About Prayer* (Portland, OR: Multnomah Press, 1975), 105.

15. Quoted in Warren, *The Practice of Prayer*, 9.

16. Jim Cymbala, *Breakthrough Prayer: The Power of Connecting with the Heart of God* (Grand Rapids, MI: Zondervan, 2003), 18.

17. Kathleen Norris, *Dakota, A Spiritual Geography* (New York: Houghton Mifflin, 1993), 184.

18. Quoted in T.M. Moore, *The Psalms for Prayer* (Grand Rapids, MI: Baker Books, 2002), 9.

19. Walter Brueggemann, quoted in John Goldingay, *Do We Need the New Testament? Letting the Old Testament Speak for Itself* (Downers Grove, IL: InterVarsity Press, 2015), 108.

20. Peterson, *Answering God*, 7.

21. Rick Stedman, *Praying the Promises of Jesus* (Eugene, OR: Harvest House Publishers, 2016).

22. Timothy Keller with Kathy Keller, *The Songs of Jesus: A Year of Daily Devotions in the Psalms* (New York: Viking, 2015), ix.

23. Nosson Scherman, *The Complete ArtScroll Siddur: A New Translation and Commentary* (Brooklyn, NY: Mesorah Publications, Ltd., 1985), xi.

24. Dietrich Bonhoeffer, *Psalms: The Prayer Book of the Bible* (Minneapolis, MN: Augsburg Publishing, 1970), 13.

25. Peterson, *Answering God*, 3.

26. Leah Libresco, *Arriving at Amen: Seven Catholic Prayers that Even I Can Offer* (Notre Dame, IN: Ave Maria Press, 2015), 91.

27. Ellen T. Charry, *Psalms 1-50, Brazos Theological Commentary on the Bible* (Grand Rapids, MI: Brazos Press, 2015).

Chapter 2: Does God Care About Emotions? (Psalm 1)

1. G.K. Chesterton, *St. Francis of Assisi* (New York: Doubleday, 1957), 67.

2. *Today in the Word*, June 1988, 13.

3. Ernest Mehew, ed., *Selected Letters of Robert Louis Stevenson* (New Haven, CT: Yale University Press, 1997), 110.

4. Stedman, *Praying the Promises of Jesus*, 50-51.

5. Elton Trueblood, *The Humor of Jesus* (San Francisco: Harper and Row, 1964), 15.

6. Henry David Thoreau, *Walden* (New York: New American Library of World Literature, 1960), 10.

7. Gerhard Kittel, Gerhard Friedrich, and Geoffrey W. Bromley, eds., "Makarios," *Theological Dictionary of the New Testament, Abridged in One Volume* (Grand Rapids, MI: Wm. B. Eerdmans Publishing Co., 1985), 548-49.

8. Some of the content of this chapter is excerpted from Stedman, *Praying the Promises of Jesus*, used by permission of Harvest House Publishers.

9. Dennis Prager, *Happiness Is a Serious Problem* (New York: Harper Collins Publishers, 1998), xi.

10. Rick Stedman, *31 Surprising Reasons to Believe in God* (Eugene, OR: Harvest House, 2017).

11. Philip Yancey, *Prayer: Does It Make Any Difference?* (Grand Rapids, MI: Zondervan, 2006), 167, 173.

12. *Ash-er-ey* is from the Hebrew root *ash-ar*, meaning "straight," "right," and thus "happy," and before Psalms and Proverbs *ash-er-ey* is never translated "blessed" in the NIV, but instead is translated "happy." Suddenly, in the Psalms, *ash-er-ey* is translated "blessed" thirty-six times and "happy" only twice.

    In addition, the most common Hebrew root word behind "bless," "blessing(s)," and "blessed" is *bah-rach* (the root meaning of which is "to kneel"). Before the Psalms, in the NIV, the verbs "bless" and "blesses" are almost always a translation of *bah-rach* (over 100 times) and only twice of *ash-er-ey*. The same is true of *bah-rach* in its adjectival form, "blessing" (70 to 1). It is only in the Wisdom Literature (Psalms, Proverbs, etc.) that *ash-er-ey* suddenly replaces *bah-rach* as the noun most frequently translated "blessed" (36 to 13).

    In other words, until the Psalms, in the NIV, "blessed" translated the noun from the root "to kneel" whereas "happy" translated the noun from the root "straight, right, happy." Yet suddenly in the Psalms, both words were translated as "blessed." Why was "happy" dropped? I know of no historical reason for this change, so I chalk it up to translators' prejudice: they simply were not comfortable with such an emotional sounding word. I conclude that "happy" is indeed the preferable translation of *ash-er-ey.*

13. I thank my administrative assistant, Lori Clark (to whom this book is dedicated), who meticulously gathered this data, and who also compiled the lists in appendix 2.

14. Daniel Goleman, *Emotional Intelligence: Why It Can Matter More than IQ* (New York: Bantam Books, 1995), 57.

15. Sigmund Freud, quoted in Daniel Goleman, *Working with Emotional Intelligence* (New York: Bantam Dell, 1998), 135.

16. Kathleen Norris, *Amazing Grace: A Vocabulary of Faith* (New York: Riverhead Books, 1998), 62.

17. Blaise Pascal, *Pensées* (London: Penguin Group, 1995), 127.

18. The word *stream* was added to this list of emotionally laden phrases in Psalm 1 by one of my early draft readers, who noted: "The writer did not choose 'lake' or 'moat,' but he used something *flowing*, which suggests life and energy." For this reader, a flowing stream provoked positive emotions. After hearing his insight, I added it to my list (thanks, Nicholas).

19. Several years ago I wrote a book on the positive side of single sexuality, that is, the

positive side of chastity outside marriage. Rick Stedman, *Your Single Treasure* (Chicago: Moody Press, 1993, 2000).

20. E Michael Jones, *Monsters from the Id* (Dallas, TX: Spence Publishing, 2000).

21. F. Delitzsch, *Psalms, Volume V, Commentary on the Old Testament in Ten Volumes* (Grand Rapids, MI: Wm. B. Eerdmans Publishing Co., reprinted 1978), 85.

22. Mitchell Dahood, *Psalms I: 1-50, The Anchor Bible,* vol. 16 (Garden City, NY: Doubleday, 1965), 3.

Chapter 3: Is God an Emotional Being? (Psalm 2)

1. Goleman, *Working with Emotional Intelligence*, 56.

2. Though scholars are unsure of the meaning of *Selah*, three leading proposals are: (1) a musical notation such as "pause" or "louder"; (2) "forever"; and (3) the point in worship in which the congregation prostrated themselves. See Peter C. Craigie, *Psalms 1-50, Word Biblical Commentary,* vol. 19 (Waco, TX: Word Books, 1983), 76-77.

3. I love Warren Wiersbe's insight: "The secret of waiting is the heart. *It takes as much courage to wait as it does to war.*" Wiersbe, *Meet Yourself in the Psalms* (Wheaton, IL: Victor Books, 1983), 118, italics not added.

4. Shoshana Zuboff, quoted in Goleman, *Working with Emotional Intelligence*, 61.

5. Goleman, *Emotional Intelligence*, 36.

6. Goleman, *Working with Emotional Intelligence*, 17.

7. Ibid., 45.

8. Ibid., 33-34.

9. Goleman, *Emotional Intelligence,* 34.

10. I am indebted to Ken Logan, PsyD, for this insight.

11. I am indebted to Jennifer Hoffman, MA, MFT, for this insight.

12. Goleman, *Emotional Intelligence,* 42-44.

13. Ibid., 289.

14. Ibid.

15. Ibid., 289-90.

16. Mario Mikulincer and Phillip R. Shaver, "Attachment Theory and Emotions in Close Relationships," *Personal Relationships* 12 (2005): 149.

17. C.S. Lewis, *Reflections on the Psalms* (Glasgow: William Collins Sons, 1961), 30-31.

18. Ray C. Stedman gives this definition of God's wrath: "According to the Scriptures, the wrath of God is God's moral integrity." Stedman, *Folk Songs of Faith* (Glendale, CA: Regal Books, 1973), 245.

19. Neil Clark Warren, *Make Anger Your Ally* (Colorado Springs, CO: Focus on the Family Publishing, 1990), 113-14.

20. Goleman, *Emotional Intelligence,* 50.

21. Walter Brueggemann, *Praying the Psalms* (Eugene, OR: Cascade Books, 2007), 55.

22. Aristotle, *De Anima*, Book III, 4-5.

23. On the other hand, for an impassioned defense of the doctrine of divine impassibility, see David Bentley Hart, *The Beauty of the Infinite* (Grand Rapids, MI: Wm. B. Eerdmans Publishing Co., 2003), 155-82).

24. Tim Clinton and Joshua Straub, *God Attachment: Why You Believe, Act, and Feel the Way You Do About God* (New York: Howard Books, 2010), 180-82.

25. Technically, the "son" in Psalm 2:7 is the Davidic king and dynasty, which is itself a part of the sonship arising out of the Sinai covenant between God and Israel. But this does not negate any feelings of sonship on the part of the psalmist nor for those reading this psalm in worship. The psalmist would share in the *sonship* identity of all Israelites, which is why Jews to this day are called *sons of the covenant*. See Craigie, *Psalms 1-50*, 67.

Chapter 4: Building a Secure Attachment with God (Psalms 3 and 4)

1. Joe Beam, *Becoming One: Emotionally, Physically, Spiritually* (West Monroe, LA: Howard Publishing, 1999), 46.

2. Emotionally Focused Therapy is one expression of the therapeutic approaches that have developed out of Bowlby's attachment theories. Others include Imago Therapy, Safe Haven Counseling, and Gottman Method Couple's Therapy.

3. L. Greenberg and S.M. Johnson, *Emotionally Focused Therapy for Couples* (New York: Guilford Press, 1988).

4. Parents need great wisdom to attune with their children, yet at the same time not overindulge them. Such wisdom will involve lots of trial and error and will apply differently to each child. In sum, "appropriately emotionally present" does not mean always giving in to a child's whims and demands. Children need to learn boundaries and independence also. Parenthood is a relational art, not a science.

5. John Bowlby, quoted in Tim Clinton and Gary Sibcy, *Attachments: Why You Love, Feel and Act the Way You Do* (Brentwood, TN: Thomas Nelson, 2002), 15.

6. Archibald Hart and Sharon Hart May, *Safe Haven Marriage* (Nashville, TN: Thomas Nelson, 2003).

7. Amir Levine, MD, and Rachel S.F. Heller, MA, *Attached: The New Science of Adult Attachment and How It Can Help You Find—and Keep—Love* (New York: Penguin Group, 2010), 33.

8. C.H. Spurgeon, *The Treasury of David*, vol. 1, *Psalm I to XXVI* (McLean, VA: MacDonald Publishing Company), 22.

9. Roy Zuck, quoted in John Hull and Tim Elmore, *Pivotal Praying: Connecting with God in Times of Great Need* (Nashville, TN: Thomas Nelson, 2002), 16-17.

10. Susan S. Phillips, *The Cultivated Life: From Ceaseless Striving to Receiving Joy* (Downers Grove, IL: InterVarsity Press, 2015), 143.

11. Craigie, *Psalms 1-50*, 74.

12. Brian Dodd makes a case (agreeing with James Barr) against the translation of *Abba* as "Daddy." I agree and have always felt that calling God "Daddy" in prayer was inappropriate, like calling my own father by his first name. Thus, I use "Father" in this prayer. Dodd, *Praying Jesus' Way*, 58-59. But my favorite story about those who address God as "Daddy" in public prayers concerns a woman who scolded her pastor for calling God "Daddy" in his pastoral prayer. He defended himself by saying, "Jesus did it." Her response was, "Well, you're not Jesus."

Chapter 5: Connecting with God Through Anger, Grief, and Sadness (Psalms 5 and 6)

1. Isaac Bashevis Singer, quoted in Peterson, *Answering God*, 36.

2. I believe Paul's admonition in Ephesians 4:29 should still govern our verbal behavior: "Do not let any unwholesome talk come out of your mouths." This would disallow, in my opinion, provocative speech such as the title of a scholarly article about the imprecatory Psalms (see http://btb.sagepub.com/content/13/4/116.extract). Knowledge is not license.

3. Lewis, *Reflections on the Psalms*, 113.

4. Dan B. Allender and Tremper Longman III, *The Cry of the Soul: How Our Emotions Reveal Our Deepest Questions About God* (Colorado Springs, CO: NavPress, 1994, 2015), 19.

5. Brueggemann, *Praying the Psalms*, 64-65.

6. H. Norman Wright, *Recovering from the Losses of Life* (Grand Rapids, MI: Fleming H. Revell, 1991, 1993), 14,16.

7. Clinton and Sibcy, *Attachments*, 260.

8. Elizabeth Backfish, "'My God Is a Rock in a Weary Land': A Comparison of the Cries and Hopes of the Psalms and African American Slave Spirituals," in *Christian Scholar's Review* 13 (Fall 2012): 21.

9. "Rivers of Babylon," written by Brent Dowe and Trevor McNaughton (1970); recorded by Boney M on *Nightflight to Venus* (1978 album).

10. Before we proceed, take a moment to join over seven million viewers who have watched the group perform this song at www.youtube.com/watch?v=9ybv4DOj-N0. Now that's great music!

11. Goldingay, *Do We Need the New Testament?*, 113-14.

12. Peterson, *Answering God*, 97.

13. C.S. Lewis, *Christian Reflections* (Grand Rapids, MI: Wm. B. Eerdmans Publishing Co., 1967), 114,116.

14. Goldingay, *Do We Need the New Testament?*, 114.

15. Allender and Longman, *Cry of the Soul*, 14.

16. Peter Scazzero with Warren Bird, *The Emotionally Healthy Church* (Grand Rapids, MI: Zondervan, 2003), 26.

17. Ibid., 22.

18. Ibid., 71.

19. Scazzero, *Emotionally Healthy Spirituality*, 15.

20. Scazzero, *Emotionally Healthy Church*, 28.

21. The part of Scazzero's story that I don't relate with is the cursing, but the credit for this is not mine. I was raised in a home completely without cursing, which will sound astonishing to many people in our culture. I have never heard either of my parents utter a curse word. Their example created a great strength within me, though occasionally I fall short of their perfect record. One day, in the kitchen with one of our kids who was home from college, I said, "Damn!" My son was shocked to hear such a word from my lips. I excused it by claiming, "Well, I was only quoting Scripture," but I later withdrew that comment and apologized.

22. Scazzero, *Emotionally Healthy Church*, 21.

23. Ibid., 19.

24. Dan Allender and Tremper Longman III, *Bold Love* (Colorado Springs, CO: NavPress, 1992), 199-200.

25. Resources that deal with sorrow, loss, and grief recovery that my wife or I have found helpful include: Nicholas Wolterstorff, *Lament for a Son* (Grand Rapids, MI: Wm. B. Eerdmans Publishing Co., 1987); H. Norman Wright, *Recovering from the Losses of Life* (Grand Rapids, MI: Fleming H. Revell, 1991, 1993); C.S. Lewis, *A Grief Observed* (New York: Crosswicks, 1961, 1989); Philip Yancey, *Where Is God When It Hurts?* (Grand Rapids, MI: Zondervan, 1977, 1990); Jurgen Moltmann, *The Crucified God* (New York: Harper and Row, 1975); Charles Ohlrich, *The Suffering God: Hope and Comfort to Those Who Hurt* (Downers Grove, IL: InterVarsity Press, 1975); *GriefShare: Your Journey from Mourning to Joy* (Wake Forest, NC: Church Initiative, 2006).

26. Bonhoeffer, *The Psalms*, 26.

Chapter 6: Does God Feel Loved by Me? (Psalms 7 and 8)

1. Sebastian Moore, quoted in Kathleen Norris, *The Cloister Walk* (New York: Riverhead Books, 1996), 91.

2. Scot McKnight, quoted in Adam S. McHugh, *The Listening Life* (Downers Grove, IL: InterVarsity Press, 2015), 18.

3. The phrase, "feel felt," I first read in an article excerpt given to Amy and me by our therapist. The paper is by Karl D. Lehman, MD, and Charlotte E.T. Lehman, MDiv, "Brain Science, Emotional Trauma, and the God Who Is with Us, Part II: The Processing Pathway for Painful Experiences and the Definition of Psychological Trauma" (revised 2011), which can be found at: www.kclehman.com/index.php?view=new_BrainScienceSeminarDocuments2007-2008.

4. Goleman, *Working with Emotional Intelligence*, 135-36.

5. Ken Hughes, quoted in Ohlrich, *The Suffering God*, 93.

6. Allender and Longman, *Cry of the Soul*, 21-22.

7. Richard Foster, *Prayer*, 85.

8. Dallas Willard, *The Great Omission: Reclaiming Jesus's Essential Teachings on Discipleship* (New York: HarperOne, 2006), 61,80.

9. Carl Sagan, *Pale Blue Dot* (New York: Random House, 1994), 7.

10. Richard Dawkins, *River Out of Eden* (New York: Basic Books, 1995), 112.

11. *Webster's New Collegiate Dictionary* (Springfield, MA: G and C Merriam, 1956), 125.

Chapter 7: Moving from "Why God?" to Worship (Psalms 9 and 10)

1. Annie Dillard, *Pilgrim at Tinker Creek* (New York: Harper's Magazine Press, 1974), 271.

2. Thomas Merton, *Praying the Psalms* (Collegeville, MN: The Liturgical Press), 26 (italics in the original).

3. Johann Christian Arnold, *Escape Routes* (Farmington, PA: The Plough Publishing House, 2002), 15-16.

4. Martin Luther King Jr., quoted in *Classics Devotional Bible,* New International Version (Grand Rapids, MI: Zondervan, 1996), 619.

5. Pascal, *Pensées*, 127.

6. William J. Peterson and Randy Peterson, *The One Year Book of Psalms* (Wheaton, IL: Tyndale House Publishers, 1999), January 17.

7. Stanley L. Jaki, *Praying the Psalms: A Commentary* (Grand Rapids, MI: Wm. B. Eerdmans Publishing Co., 2001), 17.

8. Allender and Longman, *Cry of the Soul,* 18-19.

9. Mother Teresa, *No Greater Love* (Novato, CA: New World Library, 1989), 8.

10. St. John of the Cross, *Ascent of Mount Carmel,* bk. 2, ch. 7, no. 11. Martin Luther expressed a similar belief: "It is God's nature to make something out of nothing; hence one who is not yet nothing, out of him God cannot make anything... Therefore God accepts only the forsaken, cures only the sick, gives sight only to the blind, restores life only to the dead, sanctifies only the sinners, gives wisdom only to the unwise. In short, He has mercy only on those who are wretched, and gives grace only to those who are not in grace." Martin Luther, "Commentary of Psalm 38," *Luther's Works,* 14:163.

11. Norris, *The Cloister Walk,* 94, 95, 96, 104.

12. The NET Bible, note on Psalm 43:1.

13. Dillard, *Pilgrim at Tinker Creek,* 271.

14. Interestingly, *halal* is also used in a negative sense of those who praise themselves. Thus, in Psalm 5:5; 73:3; and 75:4, *halal* is translated "arrogant" or "arrogance" in the NIV and even "fool" or "foolish" in the KJV. In Psalm 49:6, *halal* is found in the phrase, "those who boast of their great riches."

15. Goleman, *Working with Emotional Intelligence,* 243.

16. Merton, *Praying the Psalms,* 12-13.

17. Goleman, *Emotional Intelligence,* 57.

18. Ibid., 64.

Acknowledgments

As the Psalms are chock-full of the emotion of thankfulness, so was the life of Jesus. He told parables that involved gratitude and gave thanks to God repeatedly: after the miracles of the loaves and fishes, after the raising of Lazarus, and even near the end of his life at the Last Supper. Jesus was a thankful man.

Therefore, like the Master himself, I would like to end this book by giving thanks.

- First and foremost, I thank my wife, Amy, the love of my life and my companion on the quest for emotional maturity. Plus, Amy's MS in counseling from Cal State Fullerton gives her great depth and knowledge in psychological matters. Thanks also to our three children, Micah, Noah, and Jesse, who own the deepest places of love and emotions in our hearts.

- Thanks to my parents, Don and Gay Stedman, siblings Randy and Teri, and in-laws, Dean and Marcia Holst. These key people in my life are consistent sources of love and encouragement to me.

- I also thank our extended family spread across the nation, many of whom Amy and I were able to visit on a coast-to-coast-and-backroad trip we took in the spring of 2015. Our adventure involved forty days, twenty-nine states, over eighty family members, ten thousand miles driven, two oil changes, and thirty mpg average. But the best part was the visits. Thanks to you all who opened your hearts and homes to us—I only wish we all lived closer and could spend more time together. That would be—and someday will literally be—heaven.

- Thanks to my church edit team members, who once again tremendously helped me wordsmith each page and correct my many mistakes. Thanks especially to Nicholas Domich, Bev Graham, Vivian Jones, Lori Clark, Erik Neilson, and Debra Sykes. Thanks also to these counseling professionals who gave me their "counsel" on this book: Kenneth Logan, PsyD, John Branderhorst, MA, MFT, Jennifer Hoffman, MA, MFT, and my precious wife, Amy Stedman, MA (in counseling).

- A double thanks is due to Lori Clark, my angelic assistant for over nineteen years. She helped me immensely and over the years deeply blessed my family.

- Thanks also to my literary agent, Janet Grant, and to the team at Harvest House, including Terry Glaspey, Rod Morris, and Steve Miller, for their help with this book and the others in this prayer trilogy. I pray God will use our efforts to help Christians improve their prayer lives and to assist pastors to better train their congregations in prayer.

- Thanks also to our dear church, Adventure Christian Church of Roseville, California, for your love and support over the twenty-one years I was blessed to be your senior pastor. Serving God in this church was an honor beyond measure. I will forever give God thanks for the love you all showed me and my family, as well as the tens of thousands of lives that together we were able to impact for our King.

- Above all I thank that King, our Lord and Savior Jesus Christ, who modeled not only thankfulness but what a fully mature and healthy emotional life looks like. Jesus was the perfect embodiment of all the fruits of the Spirit, which are simply emotions as they were originally created by God to function in our lives. If this book helps followers of Jesus grow in these emotional attributes, that will be yet another reason to give God thanks.

About the Author

Dr. Rick Stedman is a collector of classic rock-and-roll vinyl LPs, bookaholic, author, philosopher, pastor, and devoted husband and father. For two decades he led Adventure Christian Church in Roseville, California, a church that he founded and that in the first ten years grew from zero to five thousand (in spite of the fact that Rick listens to his records as he writes his sermons).

Rick has graduate degrees in theology, philosophy, and ministry, and has been a guest on various radio shows, including *Focus on the Family*. For relaxation he likes to read, listen to his records, ride on his tractor, tinker in his workshop, and watch movies with his wife and best friend, Amy.

Rick has also written *Praying the Armor of God* and *Praying the Promises of Jesus*, books that with this one form a prayer trilogy. He is now writing a series of books on apologetics, and also is the author of *Your Single Treasure: The Good News about Singles and Sexuality*, which has been in print for over twenty years.

Further resources on prayer as well as access to Rick's blog are available at rickstedman.com, and Rick can be reached personally at rick@rickstedman.com.